ISRAEL 2016 HUMAN RIGHTS REPORT

EXECUTIVE SUMMARY

Israel is a multiparty parliamentary democracy. Although it has no constitution, parliament, the unicameral 120-member Knesset, has enacted a series of "Basic Laws" that enumerate fundamental rights. Certain fundamental laws, orders, and regulations legally depend on the existence of a "state of emergency," which has been in effect since 1948. Under the Basic Laws, the Knesset has the power to dissolve the government and mandate elections. The nationwide Knesset elections in 2015, considered free and fair, resulted in a coalition government led by Prime Minister Benjamin Netanyahu. An annex to this report covers human rights in the occupied territories. This report deals with human rights in Israel and the Israeli-occupied Golan Heights.

Civilian authorities maintained effective control over the security services. During the year, according to the Ministry of Foreign Affairs, Palestinians committed 12 terror attacks within the Green Line that led to the deaths of seven Israelis and one foreign citizen, as well as injuries to 62 Israelis. According to the Ministry of Foreign Affairs, Palestinian militants fired 46 projectiles into Israel, and there were 21 incidents of mortar fire or cross-border shooting from Syria. Further information on the human rights situation in the occupied territories is in the annex.

The most significant human rights problems were terrorist attacks targeting civilians and politically and religiously motivated societal violence; institutional and societal discrimination against Arab citizens of Israel, many of whom self-identify as Palestinian, in particular in access to equal education, housing, and employment opportunities; and institutional and societal discrimination against Ethiopian Israelis and women.

Other human rights problems included administrative detention, often extraterritorial in Israel, of Palestinians from the occupied territories; stigmatizing of human rights nongovernmental organizations (NGOs); the treatment of asylum seekers and irregular migrants; institutional and societal discrimination against non-Orthodox Jews and intermarried families; and labor rights abuses against Arab and foreign workers.

The government took some steps to prosecute and punish officials who committed abuses within Israel regardless of rank or seniority.

Section 1. Respect for the Integrity of the Person, Including Freedom from:

a. Arbitrary Deprivation of Life and other Unlawful or Politically Motivated Killings

There were reports the government or its agents committed arbitrary or unlawful killings.

The number of terrorist attacks by armed individuals decreased during the year, while attacks by rocket and mortar fire increased. According to the Ministry of Foreign Affairs, militant groups launched 46 projectiles from the Gaza Strip, and there were 21 incidents of mortar fire or cross-border firing from Syria.

The wave of uncoordinated attacks, which began in September 2015, mostly by lone attackers not directed by any organization, decreased during the year. According to the Ministry of Foreign Affairs, during the year terrorist attacks killed eight persons and injured 62. Inside the Green Line, the location of attacks included West Jerusalem, Tel Aviv-Jaffa, Netanya, Petah Tikva, Rahat, and Ramle. Most of the attackers were Palestinians from the West Bank, and four were Arab citizens of Israel. A much higher number of attacks occurred in the West Bank and Jerusalem (see annex).

For example, a bar on Dizengoff Street in Tel Aviv was the site of an attack on January 1, when Arab citizen of Israel Nashat Milhem killed two persons, injured eight others, and later killed a taxi driver. Security forces killed Milhem after a weeklong hunt.

On June 8, Palestinian cousins Khaled and Mahmoud Mahamrah fired on customers in a Tel Aviv marketplace, killing four Israelis. Authorities captured the two gunmen and indicted them for murder on July 4 in Tel Aviv District Court. Authorities indicted Yunis Aish Musa Zin, from the same West Bank town, on charges of aiding and abetting a terrorist attack. The cases continued as of the end of the year.

On October 25, the Egyptian military shot and killed 15-year-old Arab citizen of Israel Nimer Abu Amer, who was accompanying relatives employed in maintenance work on the border fence between Israel and Egypt by a contractor for the Ministry of Defense. An investigation was underway as of November 1.

b. Disappearance

There were no reports of politically motivated disappearances.

c. Torture and Other Cruel, Inhuman, or Degrading Treatment or Punishment

The law does not refer to a specific crime of torture but prohibits acts such as assault and pressure by a public official. In 1999 the Supreme Court ruled that although torture and the application of physical or psychological pain were illegal, Israeli Security Agency (ISA) interrogators might be exempt from criminal prosecution if they used such methods in extraordinary cases determined to involve an imminent threat, the "ticking bomb" scenario. Human rights organizations such as the Public Committee Against Torture in Israel (PCATI), Defense for Children International-Palestine, and Military Court Watch reported that "physical interrogation methods" permitted by Israeli law and used by security personnel could amount to torture. The methods included beatings, forcing an individual to hold a stress position for long periods, and painful pressure from shackles or restraints applied to the forearms. The government insisted it did not use any interrogation methods prohibited by the UN Convention Against Torture (UNCAT).

NGOs continued to criticize other alleged detention practices they termed abusive, including isolation, sleep deprivation, unnecessary shackling, denying access to legal counsel, and psychological abuse such as threats to interrogate family members or demolish family homes.

In May a report in the newspaper *Ha'aretz* alleged that Israeli soldiers abused three Palestinian minors from Gaza for three days after their arrest in October 2015. The abuse included being stripped, kicked, sleep deprived, beaten with a rifle butt, and burned with cigarette butts. After the three minors completed sentences of four to six months, authorities released them from prison and returned them to Gaza. The Israeli Defense Force (IDF) stated that the allegations were under investigation by the Military Advocate General.

The government established the Turkel Commission to implement the findings of the 2010 report of the Public Commission to Examine the Maritime Incident--the interception and capture by the Israeli Navy of ships carrying humanitarian aid bound for Gaza. Following the publication of the Turkel Commission's Second Report in 2013, which examined the country's mechanisms for investigating alleged violations of the laws of war, the government in 2014 established a team of professionals led by Joseph Ciechanover to recommend practical steps to implement the recommendations of that report.

The Ciechanover report, released in September 2015, found that overall the country's internal mechanisms for investigating and prosecuting alleged war crimes, many initiated following and in response to the Turkel Commission report, were sufficient and unbiased. Civil society groups criticized the Ciechanover Commission for deferring a decision to impose responsibility on military commanders and civilian superiors for offenses committed by their subordinates. The Ciechanover Commission opted instead to recommend that: "[T]he question of the explicit anchoring of the responsibility of military commanders and civilian superiors in Israeli law would continue to be examined by the relevant parties before being decided." The report also recommended increasing and clarifying civilian oversight (via the attorney general) of the military justice system. In July the security cabinet adopted the report's recommendations. In the context of the Ciechanover report, and in response to more than 60 complaints of soldier violence that the military closed without response from 2014 to September, the Supreme Court ruled in September that complaints should be examined within 14 weeks.

Authorities continued to state the ISA held detainees in isolation only in extreme cases and when there was no alternative option and that it did not use isolation as a means of augmenting interrogation, forcing a confession, or as punishment. The government rejected claims that interrogations of minors breached the convention, claiming that reforms implemented since 2008 improved the treatment of Palestinian minors, including the establishment of a Juvenile Military Court, raising the age of majority to 18 years old, introducing a special statute of limitation for minors, improving notification to a minor's family and the minors themselves regarding their rights, and reducing detention periods (see annex). An independent Inspector for Complaints Against ISA Interrogators in the Ministry of Justice handled complaints of misconduct and abuse in interrogations.

In contrast to criminal cases investigated by police for crimes with a maximum imprisonment of 10 years or more, in which regulations require recording interrogations, an extended temporary law exempts the General Security Services from audio and video recording of interrogations of "security suspects." The Ciechanover report recommended installing cameras in all ISA interrogation rooms that broadcast to a control room in real time, via closed-circuit. The government's implementation team recommended locating this control room in an ISA facility where interrogations are not conducted and that it be accessible and available to a supervising entity from the Ministry of Justice at any time. According to the recommendation, the supervising entity will prepare a concise memorandum on what the observer saw, but no other record will be kept. In the event that the supervising entity believes that interrogators used illegal means during the interrogation, the observer must report the matter to the Inspector for Complaints against ISA Interrogators in the Ministry of Justice. Human rights NGOs, criticizing this mechanism as insufficient to prevent and identify torture since there is no recording of interrogations for later accountability and judicial review, submitted a petition to the Supreme Court opposing it in June 2015. The case continued as of November 7.

According to PCATI, despite more than 800 complaints of torture by detainees in Israel since 2001--in 15 percent of which cases the government acknowledged that the torture took place--the government had never brought criminal charges against an interrogator. Authorities had never indicted an ISA interrogator for torture during an investigation, but they stated every complaint was investigated and reviewed at the level of the deputy state prosecutor, at a minimum. Some complaints led to disciplinary action. PCATI reported 41 new cases of alleged torture as of September 13.

The UN Committee Against Torture, in its May review of the country's compliance with UNCAT, recommended, among 50 other recommendations, that the government provide for independent medical examinations for all detainees. PCATI added that medical personnel should be trained and equipped to identify, document, and report all allegations and evidence of torture.

PCATI stated the government's system for investigating allegations of mistreatment of detainees was complex and fragmented. For example, allegations against police and the ISA are investigated by two separate departments of the Police Investigation Department in the Ministry of Justice State Attorney's Office, with different procedures. The National Prison Wardens Investigation Unit is responsible for investigating allegations against members of the Israel Prison Service (IPS). PCATI reported that this fragmentation created a disorganized system characterized by widely varying response times and professional standards. PCATI noted that victims often did not know the institutional affiliations of the perpetrators and that complaints were often passed from one organization to another for months or years, each authority denying jurisdiction in the case.

In December 2015 the Supreme Court rejected an appeal by prisoners under questioning for alleged involvement in a terror attack in Duma, the West Bank, in

July 2015. The prisoners' lawyer claimed the ISA prevented the prisoners from meeting with a lawyer and alleged ISA interrogators used illegal methods against the prisoners, including physical force and sleep deprivation. The Association for Civil Rights in Israel called on the Ministry of Justice to investigate the allegations. The Ministry of Justice took no action during the year.

The ISA reported the number of hate crimes by Jews dropped significantly after the Duma attack, including only one in the first eight months of the year, compared with 14 hate crimes in 2015 prior to the attack. A September report by *Ha'aretz* alleged that the government denied legal counsel to dozens of Jews arrested by the ISA in recent years for up to three weeks, which their lawyers claimed unfairly targeted settlers.

On May 22, plainclothes Border Police officers beat an Arab citizen of Israel, Maysam Abu Alqian, outside the supermarket where he was working in central Tel Aviv. After requesting to see his identification, the officers beat Alqian severely. The officers later alleged that he attacked them, but the Tel Aviv District Court ordered him released the day after his arrest. On May 31, police internal investigations unit announced that they were investigating the incident. As of November 4, the case remained under investigation.

The government's investigation into the death of Palestinian prisoner Arafat Jaradat, who died in custody at Megiddo Prison in 2013, concluded in August 2015 when a judge ruled that the cause of death was uncertain, after taking into account differing forensic opinions. He ruled that most of the bruises were likely caused by resuscitation efforts and that the other bruises did not lead to Jaradat's death.

Prison and Detention Center Conditions

The law provides prisoners and detainees the right to conditions that do not harm their health or dignity. Conditions in permanent detention facilities run by the IPS generally met international standards, according to the International Commission of the Red Cross (ICRC), but an Israel Bar Association inspection visit at Neve Tirza, a women's prison, revealed major flaws, including unacceptable physical conditions, misuse of solitary confinement, and violence against prisoners. African migrants and asylum seekers detained in the Holot detention facility complained of severe cold in winter, heat in summer, and poor food quality. According to the Ministry of Foreign Affairs, authorities provided detainees with a bed, clothes, clean towels, food, free medical care, and air-conditioned living quarters. The facility offered classes and professional training, and detainees received a monthly allowance of 480 shekels ($127). NGOs reported, however, that very few detainees participated in the classes, and authorities regularly docked detainees' monthly allowance for minor infractions.

Since 2014 NGOs have had access to Holot, and in September the government reported that five NGOs visited the facility on a periodic basis. The NGO Hotline for Refugees and Migrants (HRM) reported its representatives could access Saharonim Prison by providing authorities with the name and prison identification number of the detainee who had requested their assistance, but they could not move about and engage with individuals in the facility freely and, therefore, could not obtain new detainees' names and prison numbers. The Office of the UN High Commissioner for Refugees (UNHCR) reported it could regularly access Saharonim, Givon, and Holot detention facilities by submitting a request in advance. The ICRC reported that the IPS granted it access to protected persons, including migrants in detention.

There were reports of mistreatment and abuse by Nachshon, the IPS transportation unit. For example, in May *Ha'aretz* reported that Nachshon prevented prisoners from drinking water or using the toilet for 11 hours during a routine transfer from Ramle to a prison in northern Israel. The guards provided them with a sandwich. According to the report, these circumstances forced some of the prisoners to urinate in the transport vehicle, after which all the prisoners sat in the urine for the remainder of the trip.

<u>Physical Conditions</u>: As of December 18, according to the government, there were 9,555 prisoners in IPS facilities in Israel and the occupied territories who were citizens of Israel, 10,488 prisoners who were residents, and 6,599 Palestinian prisoners. As of September 8, the government reported 49 minors who were citizens or residents of Israel and 77 Palestinian minors. Of the total prisoner population, 6,815 were characterized as security prisoners as of December 18. These prisoners often faced harsher conditions than those of the general prison population, including increased incidence of administrative detention, restricted family visits, ineligibility for temporary furloughs, and solitary confinement. According to an interministerial team established to address racism against Israelis of Ethiopian origin, the percentage of minors of Ethiopian origin in prison was nearly 10 times their proportion of the population, comprising 18.5 percent of the inmates in Ofek Prison for juveniles as of June. Data from the Public Defender's Office, reported by *Ha'aretz* in September, revealed that the proportion of Ethiopian Israeli minors convicted of crimes sentenced to prison instead of treatment was nearly 90 percent, which was three times the percentage for non-

Ethiopian Jewish minors and almost double that of minors who are Arab citizens of Israel. The publication *+972 Magazine* reported in September that it obtained data indicating 60 percent of the prisoners in Israeli prisons were Arab.

In response to a petition by the Association of Civil Rights in Israel (ACRI), in January the Supreme Court ordered the government to explain within 120 days why the average prison cell size was less than 43 square feet. According to ACRI, the average size was 32 square feet. The government replied that it would take steps to decrease the number of prisoners, thereby increasing the average living space per prisoner. A follow-up hearing was scheduled for February 2017.

In 2015 the Knesset passed a law authorizing force-feeding of hunger-striking prisoners under specific conditions; however, the Israel Medical Association declared the legislation unethical and urged doctors to refuse to implement it. Security prisoners organized several open-ended hunger strikes during the year to demand the government end administrative detention and to protest prison conditions. Mohammad al-Qiq, a Palestinian journalist detained on suspicion of affiliation and contact with Hamas, ended a 94-day hunger strike in February after authorities agreed not to extend his administrative detention past May 21. Authorities placed Bilal Kayed in administrative detention on June 13, just before completing a sentence of 14 and one-half years for attempted murder and membership in the Popular Front for the Liberation of Palestine, and he went on hunger strike for 71 days before reaching a similar agreement with security services in August. From July to September, brothers Mahmoud and Muhammad al-Balbul went on hunger strike for more than 70 days, and Malik al-Qadi for more than 60 days, before reaching similar agreements. Physicians for Human Rights-Israel (PHR-I) expressed strong opposition to the continuous shackling of detainees throughout their hunger strike--both hand and leg in the case of Muhammad al-Balbul--which PHR-I claimed was not based on any danger after two months of hunger striking, but rather on the government's efforts to break the strike. The government stated that the IPS reduced restraints to the minimum necessary, and it reassessed the need for restraints every few days.

On August 11, the district court in Be'er Sheva ruled that independent doctors such as PHR-I, hunger striker Bilal Kayed's authorized representative, could not examine him because the ICRC was already examining him. The ICRC noted their medical doctor assesses the overall medical condition and treatment of detainees on hunger strike but does not act in the role of a treating physician. According to PHR-I, in contravention of Israel's Law of Patient Rights, which states that a patient has the right to receive a copy of his own medical records, Barzilai Medical Center declined to provide Kayed's records, referring PHR-I instead to the IPS.

Palestinian Yasser Diab Hamdouna, 41, died in an Israeli prison on September 25. Palestinian media reported that the cause was a stroke or heart attack and accused the IPS of medical neglect. The Ministry of Foreign Affairs stated that he collapsed while exercising and was pronounced dead after receiving unsuccessful medical treatment. As of November 6, according to the ministry, nine other prisoners also died in IPS prisons: six from a heart attack or heart condition, two from suicide, and one from cancer.

NGOs reported lack of access to legal and social services in detention centers for irregular migrants. Social workers provided individual social and supportive treatment, with emphasis on identifying and providing services for trafficking victims, victims of abuse, and victims of sexual violations.

Administration: While authorities generally allowed visits from lawyers and stated that every inmate who requested to meet with an attorney was able to do so, this was not always the case. NGOs alleged authorities did not allow Palestinian detainees, including minors, access to a lawyer during their initial arrest. Travel restrictions on entry into the country affected the access of lawyers and other visitors to some Palestinian prisoners. The government granted permits to family members from the West Bank on a limited basis and restricted those entering from Gaza more severely. In November 2015 the IPS reportedly issued regulations limiting members of the Knesset (MKs) to one visit per month, but the Ministry of Foreign Affairs denied any such regulation exists.

The law allows prisoners to submit a petition to judicial authorities alleging substandard prison conditions, and the government stated that authorities investigated credible allegations of inhuman conditions, documented such investigations, and released the results publicly. The state comptroller serves as ombudsman and investigates public complaints against government institutions, including the IPS.

Independent Monitoring: The ICRC regularly monitored IPS facilities for irregular migrants, including Holot and Saharonim, and the two IDF provisional detention centers. The ICRC monitored all facilities in accordance with its standard modalities, except for urgent or isolated cases raised bilaterally with the concerned authorities (that is, relating to the composition of the visiting team and the conditions for interviews without witnesses). PCATI continued to press for structural reforms, including mandatory video recordings of interrogations. The Public Defenders' Office is officially responsible for monitoring and reporting on prison conditions, which it does every two years. The most recent report was issued in July 2015.

d. Arbitrary Arrest or Detention

The law prohibits arbitrary arrest and detention, and the government generally observed these prohibitions for all citizens. Authorities subjected non-Israeli residents of the Israeli-occupied Golan Heights to the same laws as Israeli citizens. Noncitizens of Palestinian origin detained on security grounds fell under military jurisdiction even if detained in Israel (see annex).

With regard to irregular migrants, the most recent amendment to the Prevention of Infiltration Law, passed in 2014, allows the government to detain migrants and asylum seekers who arrived after December 2014 for three months in the Saharonim Prison facility "for the purpose of identification and to explore options for relocation of the individual." The law also states that authorities must bring irregular migrants taken into detention to a hearing within five days and inform them of their rights, including the right to legal counsel. After three months in Saharonim, the government may then hold them for 12 months in Holot, a remote, semi-open facility run by the IPS. Authorities closed Holot from 10 p.m. to 6 a.m. and required daily check-in at 10 p.m. (see section 2.d.). Authorities did not confine detainees to their rooms during the night, but they could not leave the facility.

Authorities soon replaced the 1,178 Eritrean and Sudanese migrants released from the Holot facility after an August 2015 Supreme Court ruling with new 12-month detainees. In accordance with the Supreme Court decision, authorities may hold detainees for only one year without charging them with any offenses. The government barred those freed from Holot from living or working in either Tel Aviv or Eilat, where they would have supportive communities and access to the limited medical facilities and other social services available to the migrant population. In August authorities stopped summoning asylum seekers from Darfur or Sudan to Holot; however, many Darfuri detainees already in Holot were not released early.

The most recent amendment to the Prevention of Infiltration Law also allows authorities to send those who fail to renew their visas on time to Holot for up to 120 days. The Ministry of Interior provided renewal services in Tel Aviv, Be'er

Sheva, and Eilat. HRM reported that authorities required asylum seekers applying to renew their visa to provide a copy of a lease agreement and a current wage slip in support of their application, yet applicants could not obtain those documents without a visa, creating a vicious cycle. The law prohibits detention in Holot based on certain factors including age, health, gender, or other protected status. Authorities can send those who violated rules at Holot to Saharonim Prison. HRM reported that authorities sent more than half of Holot detainees to Saharonim for up to several months for various infractions.

Role of the Police and Security Apparatus

Under the authority of the prime minister, the ISA combats terrorism and espionage in the country and the occupied territories. The national police, including the border police and the immigration police, are under the authority of the Ministry of Internal Security. The IDF is responsible for external security and has no jurisdiction over Israeli citizens. ISA forces operating in the occupied territories fall under the IDF for operations and operational debriefing. The Ciechanover report (see section 1.c.) clarified that the Ministry of Justice and its investigators and the IDF and its investigators would divide investigative and prosecutorial responsibilities in incidents in which police operated under the authority of the military. Civilian authorities maintained effective control over the ISA and police forces, and the government has effective mechanisms to investigate and punish abuse and corruption. The government took steps to investigate allegations of the use of excessive force by police and military. NGOs continued to criticize the extremely low number of indictments issued relative to the number of investigations opened and the high percentage of cases closed due to investigation failures by military police. In May human rights NGO B'Tselem announced that it would no longer refer complaints to the military law enforcement system.

The Department for Investigation of Police Officers (DIPO) in the Ministry of Justice is responsible for investigating complaints against ISA bodies, including incidents involving police and the border police occurring on Israeli territory and Jerusalem and incidents taking place in the occupied territories that do not involve the use of a weapon. In 2015 DIPO reviewed more than 3,500 cases and reached decisions in 640, of which 102 cases ended in criminal indictments (leading to 87 convictions) and 85 in disciplinary proceedings. DIPO closed 974 cases without further investigation, and it closed another 843 following a preliminary examination.

Investigative responsibility for alleged abuses by the IDF, including incidents involving a weapon in which police units were operating under IDF authority in the occupied territories, remains with the Ministry of Defense in the Military Police Criminal Investigations Department. During the year authorities arrested or detained four soldiers, convicted 11 (including nine indicted in prior years), and sentenced 12 (including 10 indicted in prior years).

Human rights NGOs continued to allege that accountability mechanisms precluded serious internal investigations by the military and were marred by severe structural flaws that rendered them incapable of conducting professional investigations.

Arrest Procedures and Treatment of Detainees

Police must have warrants based on sufficient evidence and issued by an authorized official to arrest a suspect. The following applies to detainees, excluding those in administrative detention: Authorities generally informed such persons promptly of charges against them; the law allows authorities to detain suspects without charge for 24 hours prior to bringing them before a judge, with limited exceptions allowing for up to 48 hours; authorities generally respected these rights for persons arrested in the country; there was a functioning bail system, and detainees could appeal decisions denying bail; and authorities allowed detainees to consult with an attorney in a timely manner, including one provided by the government for the indigent, and to contact family members promptly.

Authorities detained most Palestinian prisoners arrested by Israeli security forces in the occupied territories extraterritorially in Israel. The government stated that the establishment of new prisons in the West Bank could adversely affect detainees' living conditions and affect local residents on whose land the new prisons would be built. Authorities prosecuted them under the Israeli military law applicable to the occupied territories, which denies many of the rights Israeli law would grant them. According to the circumstances of each case, such as the severity of the alleged offense, status as a minor, risk of escape, or other factors, authorities either granted or denied bail to noncitizens of Palestinian origin detained for security violations.

Authorities may prosecute persons detained on security grounds criminally or hold them as administrative detainees or illegal combatants, according to one of three legal regimes. First, under a temporary law on criminal procedures, repeatedly renewed since 2006, the IPS may hold persons suspected of a security offense for 48 hours prior to bringing them before a judge, with limited exceptions allowing the IPS to detain a suspect for up to 96 hours prior to bringing the suspect before the senior judge of a district court. In security-related cases, authorities may hold a person for up to 35 days without an indictment (versus 30 days for other than security-related cases), and the law allows the court to lengthen the holding of a detainee on security grounds for an initial period of up to 20 days for interrogation without an indictment (versus 15 days for other than security-related cases). Authorities may deny security detainees access to an attorney for up to 21 days under Israeli law or 60 days under military regulations.

Second, the Emergency Powers Law allows the Ministry of Defense to detain persons administratively without charge for up to six months, renewable indefinitely. As of October authorities issued administrative detention orders against 20 Israeli citizens, most of them Arabs. In 2015, following several arson attacks in Israel and the West Bank, the government announced it would expand administrative detention to Jewish extremists suspected of terrorist activity. The Ministry of Foreign Affairs reported that, as of the beginning of December, authorities issued 1,764 administrative detention orders against 1,037 Palestinian adults, 29 administrative detention orders against 19 Palestinian minors over the age of 14, and none to minors under the age of 14 years old. Additionally, authorities issued 106 administrative restraining orders against 42 Israeli adults, 42 orders against 11 Israeli minors, seven orders against Palestinian adults, and none against Palestinian minors (see annex).

Third, the Illegal Combatant Law permits authorities to hold a detainee for 14 days before review by a district court judge, deny access to counsel for up to 21 days with the attorney general's approval, and allow indefinite detention subject to twice-yearly district court reviews and appeals to the Supreme Court.

While international law allows the use of administrative detention in rare "ticking time bomb" scenarios, civil society organizations and some MKs continued to criticize the government for using it excessively, adding that the practice was undemocratic since there was no due process. The government claimed that it issued administrative detention orders "against those who plan terrorist attacks, or those who orchestrate, facilitate, or otherwise actively assist in the commission of such acts when the evidence against those individuals cannot be revealed for security reasons," and it is a preventive measure of last resort. The government said it used administrative restraining orders only "when it is necessary to protect security and order and when it is not possible to use penal measures for various reasons."

<u>Arbitrary Arrest</u>: An annual report from the Office of the Public Defender on September 4 highlighted indictments on issues of trivial importance or against persons who break the law to obtain basic needs such as food, electricity, water, or housing. In 2015 there were allegations of arbitrary arrests of Arab citizens during protests, as well as such arrests of Ethiopian-Israelis.

<u>Pretrial Detention</u>: Administrative detention continued to result in lengthy pretrial detention for security detainees, who were mostly Palestinian; some, however, were Jewish Israelis or Arab citizens of Israel. Authorities held most detainees for less than one year but held some for more than one year and a small number for more than two years.

<u>Detainees' Ability to Challenge Lawfulness of Detention before a Court</u>: An administrative detainee has the right to appeal any decision to lengthen detention to a military court of appeals and then to the Supreme Court, and both Palestinian and Jewish detainees routinely did so. The military courts may rely on classified evidence denied to detainees and their lawyers when determining whether to prolong administrative detention. There is no system whereby authorities may clear a defense team member to view classified information used to justify holding an administrative detainee. Some detained Jewish youths, alleged to belong to extremist organizations, questioned the validity of their arrest and use of administrative detention, house arrest, and administrative orders banning them from certain areas of the West Bank.

<u>Protracted Detention of Rejected Asylum Seekers or Stateless Persons</u>: The Prevention of Infiltration Law defines all irregular border crossers as "infiltrators" and permits authorities to detain irregular migrants, including asylum seekers and their children.

In 2014 the Supreme Court struck down the section of the Prevention of Infiltration Law that allowed irregular migrants, including refugees and asylum seekers, to be detained in the Holot open facility indefinitely. In August 2015 the Supreme Court set the limit at one year. This resulted in the release of 1,178 asylum seekers from Holot; authorities soon replaced them with other asylum seekers. The government may still hold irregular migrants, including refugees and asylum seekers, in Saharonim Prison for three months on arrival and then move them to Holot for 12 months. The Supreme Court's ruling affirmed the use of the Holot facility to house irregular migrants, albeit for a limited period.

Under the Law of Entry, the Ministry of Interior and police developed an outline of cooperation that allows for detention of irregular migrants, including refugees and asylum seekers living in the community and suspected of criminal activity, based on an administrative order rather than through the legal process.

e. Denial of Fair Public Trial

The law provides for an independent judiciary, and the government generally respected judicial independence. (The annex covers military court trials of Palestinians and others in the occupied territories.)

Trial Procedures

The law provides for the right to a fair public trial, and an independent judiciary generally enforced this right. Exceptions to the right for a public trial include national security concerns, protection of the interest of a minor or an individual requiring special protection, and safeguarding the identity of an accuser or defendant in a sex-offense case.

Defendants enjoy the rights to a presumption of innocence, to be informed promptly and in detail of the charges against them, to be present at their trial, to a fair and public trial without undue delay, and to adequate time and facilities to prepare their defense. They may not be compelled to testify or confess guilt and may consult with an attorney or, if indigent, have one provided at public expense. Defendants have the right to free interpretation as necessary from the moment charged through all appeals. Defendants have the right to confront witnesses against them, to present witnesses and evidence on their behalf, to access evidence held against them, and to appeal to the Supreme Court. The prosecution is under a general obligation following an indictment to provide all evidence to the defense. The government may on security grounds withhold from defense lawyers evidence it gathered but will not use in its case against the accused. The Supreme Court in civilian courts or the Court of Appeals in military courts can scrutinize the decision to withhold such evidence. The rules of evidence in cases of espionage tried in criminal court do not differ from the normal rules of evidence--no use of secret evidence is permissible.

The Ministry of Justice determined the law allows the courts to consider secret evidence in reviewing the cases of Palestinians convicted in civilian courts and granted conditional release from prison as part of a prisoner exchange and later rearrested for violating the terms of their release, because authorities considered this parole board review procedural.

On August 2, in response to the wave of attacks that began in September 2015, many perpetrated by minors, the Knesset passed a "Youth Bill" legalizing imprisonment of children as young as 12 years old if convicted of serious crimes such as murder, attempted murder, or manslaughter.

Security or military trials are open to the public, but since authorities conduct them in a military camp, members of the public require an entry permit from the military. Authorities conducted certain trials in a closed setting, not open to the public, for reasons of security or for the protection of the identity of a minor.

Military courts provide some of the procedural rights granted in civilian criminal courts, although their rates of conviction of Palestinians charged with various crimes were much higher. The evidentiary rules governing trials of Palestinians, and others subject to military law in the occupied territories, are the same as evidentiary rules in criminal cases. According to the Ministry of Justice, the law does not permit convictions based solely on confessions. The government stated that the evidentiary rules applied in military trials were the same as those applied in civilian courts and did not allow presentation of secret evidence not provided to the defendant or their counsel. Counsel may assist the accused in such trials, and a judge may assign counsel to defendants. Indigent detainees do not automatically receive free legal counsel for military trials, but almost all detainees had counsel, even in minor cases. Court indictments were read in Hebrew and, unless the defendant waived this right, in Arabic. Authorities translated all military court indictments into Arabic. At least one interpreter was present for simultaneous interpretation in every military court hearing, unless the defendant waived that right. Defendants may appeal through the Military Court of Appeals and then to the Supreme Court.

Political Prisoners and Detainees

There were no reports of civilian political prisoners or detainees. ACRI, however, petitioned the Supreme Court in 2013 regarding a practice by the ISA to call in political activists suspected of "subversive" activity for questioning under caution, meaning they might be charged with a crime. In response the government confirmed that there is a classified secret procedure that regulates Israel National Police assisting the ISA in the summoning process. As of November 4, the case was still pending with the Supreme Court.

Civil Judicial Procedures and Remedies

An independent and impartial judiciary adjudicates lawsuits seeking damages for, or cessation of, human rights violations. Administrative remedies exist, and court orders usually were enforced. By law Palestinians may file suit to obtain compensation through civil suits in some cases, even when a criminal suit is unsuccessful and the actions against them considered legal.

Property Restitution

In the 35 unrecognized villages in the Negev claimed by various Bedouin tribes, the government viewed all buildings as illegal and subject to demolition. In cases of demolitions with no agreement from the residents to relocate, the government levied fines against residents to cover expenses incurred in the course of demolitions. Many Bedouin whose residences or structures authorities subjected to demolition orders elected to self-demolish to avoid fines.

According to the NGO Negev Coexistence Forum for Civil Equality (NCF), in recent years the government approved plans for the establishment of 15 new towns and settlements in the Negev region, the vast majority intended for the Jewish population. Authorities approved plans for settlements called Hiran (see below), Daya, and Neve Gurion to replace existing Bedouin villages. Authorities planned Daya to replace the unrecognized village al-Qatamat, and Neve Gurion was to replace some houses in the recognized village of Bir Haddaj. On October 9, the government demolished seven houses in Bir Haddaj, which the NCF claimed belonged to an extended family relocated there by the government 13 years earlier. In response on October 16, approximately 1,500 participants demonstrated near the regional council of Ramat Negev. The NCF noted the Negev was sparsely populated, with only 8 percent of the population living on 60 percent of Israel's land, so there was ample room to establish new communities without razing existing ones.

In January the Supreme Court ruled again that eviction orders issued against residents of the Bedouin unrecognized village Umm al-Hiran, where they had been moved by the Israeli military regime in 1956, were valid. The NCF reported that construction work on Hiran progressed and expanded during the year, reaching to within a few yards of Bedouin houses in Umm al-Hiran, and residents suffered from the dust raised by construction. As of November a group of 30 Jewish families who planned to move to Hiran remained in mobile homes in the forest outside Umm al-Hiran while waiting to obtain the land. The government offered plots of land and cash compensation to villagers who accept resettlement to the nearby Bedouin town of Hura, three miles away, but village leaders had rejected this option because, according to the Hura local council, there was insufficient space even for natural growth in the town and because of fears it would force the villagers to abandon a more traditional rural lifestyle for an urban one, with attendant problems of drugs, crime, and disintegration of the traditional family/clan structure. Village leaders expressed openness to almost any option that would allow them to remain in place, including living side-by-side with Jewish neighbors in an expanded community. Authorities scheduled demolition of structures that would have displaced approximately 30 to 40 persons in one extended family for November 22, but the Be'er Sheva Magistrate Court postponed the demolition for a last-minute appeal, which the court denied the following day. As of November 30, the targeted villagers agreed to move to Hura and began self-demolishing in order to avoid steep fines and to reuse building materials.

Other Bedouin communities, such as Attir and al-Araqib, faced eviction due to the government's forestation plans, while a planned extension of the Cross Israel Highway will affect approximately 400 structures. In May 2015 the Supreme Court rejected Bedouins' claims of ownership of al-Araqib, a small community in the northern Negev, which the government had demolished more than 100 times since 2010. Residents of al-Araqib typically rebuild their shelters within one day of demolition. In July the Jewish National Fund worked in al-Araqib for 10 days, preparing land in four lots in preparation to plant trees in the winter.

The government noted its policy in Bedouin areas was to demolish "new vacant illegal structures" built without permits after 2010 and found in areas it determined to be state land, not belonging to any local authority. The NCF recorded 982 demolitions in 2015, down from 1,073 in 2014. Demolitions by Israeli authorities increased slightly to 365 in 2015 from 355 in 2014, while Bedouins demolished the remainder to avoid fines. In May a report from the State Comptroller stated: "The ongoing circle of construction for housing and demolition of these structures deepens the alienation of the Bedouin residents of the Negev towards the state and does not contribute to the regulation of their settlement."

The government maintained a program to encourage Bedouins to relocate from unrecognized villages to established towns by providing low-cost land and compensation for demolition of illegal structures for those willing to move to designated permanent locations. Bedouins often refused to participate in this program because they asserted that they owned the land or that the government had given them prior permission to settle in their current locations. The NCF alleged the seven government-established towns were unable to accommodate their own natural growth, much less the arrival of new residents. Court-ordered demolitions and the rejection of their designated relocation sites for reasons of overcrowding caught some residents between these policies. Additionally, many Bedouins complained that moving to government-planned towns would require them to surrender claims to land they had occupied for several generations and would separate them from their livelihood. Conversely, the government claimed it was difficult and inefficient to provide services to clusters of buildings throughout the Negev that ignored planning procedures. Some Bedouins continued to pursue legal recognition of their 3,200 claims to parcels of land based on practices of land ownership and sales predating the establishment of the state in 1948, although in all cases the Supreme Court ruled in favor of the government.

NGOs and Bedouin leaders noted that the implementation of the government plan for developing the Negev, with the resultant home demolitions and planned relocations of some Bedouin communities, continued apace in the absence of specific legislation to address Bedouin land claims. The NCF raised concerns that the policies of Minister of Agriculture and Rural Development Uri Ariel had exacerbated the gaps between recognized and unrecognized Bedouin villages.

f. Arbitrary or Unlawful Interference with Privacy, Family, Home, or Correspondence

The law prohibits such actions, and the government generally respected those prohibitions. Separate religious court systems adjudicate matters such as marriage and divorce for the Jewish, Muslim, Christian, and Druze communities. Each year an estimated 20,000 civil marriages, marriages of some non-Orthodox Jews, marriages in non-Orthodox ceremonies, marriages of a Jew to a non-Jew, or marriages of a Muslim woman to a non-Muslim must take place outside the country to be considered legal, because religious courts refuse to accept these marriages, and the country lacks a civil marriage law. Many Jewish citizens objected to exclusive Orthodox control over aspects of their personal lives. For example, the Orthodox Rabbinate did not consider to be Jewish approximately 337,000 citizens who considered themselves Jewish and who immigrated either as Jews or as family members of Jews; therefore, they may not be married or buried in Jewish cemeteries in the country. The Orthodox Rabbinate had the authority to handle divorces of any Jewish couple regardless of how they were married, as well as the divorce of any couple wherein one spouse considers him or herself to be Jewish. The government stated that 24 cemeteries in the country served immigrants not considered Jewish by the Orthodox Rabbinate. The estimated 15,000 Messianic Jews, who believe Jesus is the Messiah and consider themselves Jews, also experienced these infringements on their personal lives, since the Orthodox Rabbinate regards them as Jewish apostates. Authorities did not fully implement a law requiring the government to establish civil cemeteries.

The Law of Citizenship and Entry, which is valid through April and renewed annually, prohibits Palestinians from the West Bank or Gaza, including those who are spouses of Israeli residents or citizens, from obtaining resident status in Jerusalem or Israel unless the Ministry of Interior makes a special determination, usually on humanitarian grounds. The law allows the entry of spouses of Israelis on a "staying permit" if the male spouse is age 35 or older and the female spouse is age 25 or older. Authorities required East Jerusalem residents who relocated to forfeit their Jerusalem identification cards. The government may revoke the Jerusalem identification cards of those who have been away from Jerusalem for seven years, and the government may seek to revoke a Palestinian's Jerusalem identification card if the person obtains citizenship or residency in another country. The only way to qualify for Jerusalem residency and an identification card is to derive it from one's parents or through a spouse. There is no immigration process, and one usually may not regain Jerusalem residency if authorities revoke it. (The annex addresses revocation of identity cards for Palestinian residents of East Jerusalem in more detail.)

Section 2. Respect for Civil Liberties, Including:

a. Freedom of Speech and Press

The law generally provides for freedom of speech, including for members of the press, and the government generally respected these rights. An independent press, an effective judiciary, and a functioning democratic political system combined to promote freedom of speech and of the press.

The law, however, criminalizes calling persons "Nazis" or "fascists." The law imposes tort liability on any person who knowingly issues a public call for an economic, cultural, or academic boycott of the State of Israel and the Israeli-controlled occupied territories. Plaintiffs must prove direct economic harm to claim damages under the "antiboycott" legislation. In 2015 the Supreme Court upheld the constitutionality of this law. The law also permits the minister of finance to institute regulations imposing administrative sanctions on those calling for such a boycott, including restrictions on participating in tenders for contracts with the government and denial of government benefits.

Freedom of Speech and Expression: The law prohibits hate speech and content liable to incite to violence or discrimination on grounds of race, origin, religion, nationality, and gender. The Counterterrorism Law, which passed in June and took effect in November, criminalizes as "terrorist acts" speech supportive of terrorism, including public praise of a terrorist organization, display of symbols, expression of slogans, and "incitement." There were no convictions under the law as of the end of the year.

On July 18, the Knesset passed a law increasing the penalty for desecrating the Israeli flag from one year to three years in prison and increased the fine from the equivalent of eight dollars to 58,400 shekels ($15,500).

In cases of speech that constitute incitement to violence or hate speech, the law empowers police to limit freedom of expression.

Press and Media Freedoms: The independent media were active and expressed a wide variety of views without restriction. In December, however, ACRI published a report detailing a variety of legislative and rhetorical attacks on media throughout the year by elected officials, especially Prime Minister Netanyahu, and expressed concern about the chilling effect of these attacks on press freedom. In September 2015 the Knesset amended the public broadcasting law to prohibit journalists on public broadcasting from transmitting their own views. Subsequently, the Israel Press Council urged the government to cancel the law, saying it violated free speech. The Knesset repealed the amendment in November 2015.

In April the press freedom organization Freedom House lowered Israel's ranking from free to partly free due to "the growing impact of *Israel Hayom,* whose owner-subsidized business model endangered the stability of other media outlets, and the unchecked expansion of paid content--some of it government funded--whose nature was not clearly identified to the public."

On June 23, the Ministry of Public Security barred Nazareth-based television channel Musawa for six months claiming that the Palestinian Authority funded it. Authorities previously banned the station for six months in July 2015 when it was known as Palestine 48.

The government shut media outlets associated with the Northern Islamic Movement, following that group's ban in November 2015.

<u>Censorship or Content Restrictions</u>: All media organizations must submit to military censors any material relating to specific military issues or strategic infrastructure issues, such as oil and water supplies. Organizations may appeal the censor's decisions to the Supreme Court, and the censor may not appeal a court judgment. Whereas in the past the military censor requested prepublication review of sensitive information only from major media outlets, *Ha'aretz* reported in February that the military censor expanded the request to 30 bloggers and administrators of public Facebook pages as well.

News printed or broadcast abroad is subject to security censorship. The government did not fine newspapers or other mass media for violating censorship regulations during the year. The government regularly enacted restrictive orders on sensitive security information and required foreign correspondents, as well as local media, to abide by these orders. According to data provided by the military at the request of *+972 Magazine*, Mekomit, and the Movement for Freedom of Information, from 2011 through August, the military censor banned the publication of 1,936 articles and redacted information from 14,196 articles.

In January the State Attorney's Office sought a court order to compel the NGO Breaking the Silence to reveal the identity of an individual who served in Operation Protective Edge and who testified to the organization about alleged war crimes during the operation. Breaking the Silence claimed the investigation was politically motivated and that providing this information would effectively force the organization to ends its operations. As of the end of the year, the case remained pending at the Petah Tikva Magistrate's Court.

<u>National Security</u>: In November 2015 the government used emergency law to outlaw the Northern Islamic Movement, stating that it incited violence and alleging that it closely collaborated with Hamas and the Muslim Brotherhood. MK Ahmed Tibi and other Arab Israeli politicians stated, however, that politics appeared to have motivated the decision much more than a threat to national security. The government issued cease and desist orders to 17 related organizations.

Internet Freedom

There were no government restrictions on access to the internet. The government monitored e-mail, internet chat rooms, and the popular texting application

WhatsApp for security purposes. Internet access was widely available, and approximately 73 percent of the country's inhabitants used it regularly.

In October 2015 authorities arrested Dareen Tatour, an Arab citizen of Israel, on charges of incitement to violence, terrorism, and support for a terrorist organization as a result of the poems, pictures, and other media she posted online. Authorities imprisoned her for three months and then released her to home detention, pending the completion of legal proceedings, which were remained underway at the end of the year. Tatour claimed that translations of her Arabic postings by police were poor and distorted.

In December 2015 authorities arrested attorney Tareq Barghout, part of the legal team for an alleged teenage Palestinian terrorist, on charges of publishing material on Facebook praising terrorists and encouraging further attacks. The court released Barghout, noting that the material he posted was poorly translated from Arabic to Hebrew and that he has freedom of expression as reflected in Facebook postings.

During an outbreak of fires in November, police detained Arab citizen of Israel Anas Abudaabes for three days on suspicion of incitement after he posted a sarcastic Facebook message. The publication *+972 Magazine* reported that police had attempted to translate the message using Google Translate.

Following a reported agreement between government officials and Facebook in September to remove content that the government reported as incitement, the NGO Adalah expressed grave concern the targeted content would disproportionately affect Arab citizens. They cited research showing that 70 percent of 175,000 inciting posts in Israel in the 12 months ending May were actually made by right-wing Israeli Jews against Arabs and left-wing Jews, yet only 18 percent of those arrested for incitement-related offenses during the year were Jews. A study by the Berl Katznelson Foundation published in November reported more than six million racist expressions online in Israel in one year.

Academic Freedom and Cultural Events

The law prohibits institutions that receive government funding from engaging in commemoration of the Nakba, or "catastrophe," referring to the displacement of 80 percent of the Palestinian Arab population during Israel's 1948 War of Independence.

In June the president of Ben-Gurion University overturned a decision to award the Berelson Prize for Jewish-Arab Understanding to the NGO Breaking the Silence on the grounds that it "isn't in the national consensus." Despite the university president's decision, university lecturers awarded the NGO an alternative prize at a ceremony in November. Breaking the Silence, a group of military veterans whose goal is to end the Israeli occupation of the West Bank, was the target of intensely negative rhetoric in the national discourse during the year.

The NGO Mossawa claimed that there were no Arab employees among five cinema foundations that control the 60 million shekels ($16 million) allocated by the government for Israeli cinema, and that the government selected almost no Arabic films for funding.

b. Freedom of Peaceful Assembly and Association

The law provides for the freedoms of assembly and association, and the government generally respected these rights.

In April and May 2015, thousands of Ethiopian Israelis and their supporters gathered to protest police brutality and discrimination following the publication of a video showing police beating Ethiopian IDF soldier Demas Fekadeh in the Tel Aviv suburb of Holon. The demonstrations at some points resulted in clashes with police. The demonstration resulted in 56 officers and 12 protesters injured; authorities arrested 43 persons. Police set up a committee to investigate the events. Government officials, including the president and prime minister, met with Fekadeh and Ethiopian community representatives in the wake of the demonstrations and pledged that police would conduct a thorough and transparent investigation. The government dropped charges against one officer who apprehended Fekadeh and also against Fekadeh himself, concluding Fekadeh had not initiated the altercation. According to the NGO Tebekah, the attorney general indicated in June that he would re-examine the charges against the officer. Tebekah filed a petition with the Supreme Court to compel the attorney general to give a response to the question of re-examining the charges, and the case continued as of December 9.

The police committee created to investigate the events led to several steps toward reform in partnership with an Ethiopian Israeli NGO, including a pilot project for police body cameras, which began in August, and a new police code of conduct.

Freedom of Assembly

The law provides for this right, and the government generally respected it.

Human rights NGOs alleged that in prior years, police engaged in mass arrests of Arab protesters, claiming they did not have a permit, although Israeli law does not require one in certain circumstances, or after incitement by Israeli agents provocateurs dressed as Arabs. There were no such mass arrests during the year.

There were some instances in 2015 in which police required organizers of demonstrations to accept criminal responsibility for any disturbance or prohibited behavior by participants of the demonstration before approving a permit application. Following submission of a petition to the Supreme Court by ACRI, police agreed to eliminate this condition, and ACRI withdrew its petition.

In December 2015 the government loosened police regulations to allow the use of live fire as a first resort against protesters throwing stones or incendiary devices.

Freedom of Association

The law provides for this right, and the government generally respected it.

Israeli and Palestinian NGOs, particularly those focused on human rights problems and critical of the government, asserted that the government sought to intimidate and stop their foreign funding (see section 5). According to ACRI, the law prohibits registration of an association or a party if its goals include denial of the existence of the State of Israel or the democratic character of the state. A political party will not be registered if its goals include incitement to racism or support of an armed struggle, enemy state, or terror organization against the State of Israel.

c. Freedom of Religion

See the Department of State's *International Religious Freedom Report* at www.state.gov/religiousfreedomreport/.

d. Freedom of Movement, Internally Displaced Persons, Protection of Refugees, and Stateless Persons

The law provides for freedom of internal movement, foreign travel, emigration, and repatriation, and the government generally respected these rights for citizens.

The government cooperated with the Office of the UN High Commissioner for Refugees (UNHCR) and other humanitarian organizations in providing protection and assistance to internally displaced persons (IDPs), refugees, returning refugees, asylum seekers, stateless persons, or other persons of concern, except as noted below.

Abuse of Migrants, Refugees, and Stateless Persons: Communities with a large concentration of African migrants were occasionally targets of violence. The Tel Aviv municipality dedicated a special police unit to combat violence and crime in the migrant community. Additionally, the nature of government policies on the legality of work forced many refugees to work in "unofficial" positions, making them more susceptible to poor treatment and questionable work practices by their employers.

Immediately following the killing of a soldier by an Israeli Bedouin attacker in Beer Sheva in October 2015, a security guard shot Eritrean asylum seeker Haptom Zerhom, who the guard mistakenly believed was a second attacker. A group of onlookers then beat the injured Eritrean man, who later died. Pathologists later confirmed the cause of death was the gunshot wound. In January authorities indicted Eviatar Damari, David Moyal, soldier Yaakov Shamba, and prison officer Ronen Cohen for causing grievous bodily harm with serious intent. The case was scheduled to resume in February 2017.

Foreign Travel: Citizens generally were free to travel abroad provided they had no outstanding military obligations and no administrative restrictions. The government may bar citizens from leaving the country based on security considerations. Authorities do not permit any citizen to travel to any state officially at war with Israel without government permission. This restriction includes travel to Syria, Iraq, Iran, Lebanon, Yemen, and Saudi Arabia.

Adalah alleged that the prohibition on travel to many Arab countries disproportionately discriminated against Arab-Israeli citizens and noted that authorities did not detain Jewish Israelis upon return from similar trips to unauthorized countries. The government required all citizens to have a special permit to enter "Area A" in the West Bank (the area, according to the Interim Agreement, in which the Palestinian Authority exercises civil and security responsibility), although the government allowed Palestinian citizens access without permits. In March 2015 the Supreme Court rejected a petition by ACRI requesting the airport to eliminate racial profiling of Arab citizens.

In 2014 the Supreme Court upheld a policy that did not allow Palestinians from Gaza to enter Israel to access courts for tort damages filed against the security forces, stating that it wanted to "give a chance" to new procedures and guidelines for facilitating entry into the country adopted by the attorney general. The Ministry of Foreign Affairs stated in November that Gazans who prove that their entry into Israel is necessary for their court case to be effectively managed, and the results of the case affect a humanitarian need, are granted entry. The burden of proof remains on the plaintiff to justify the application to enter Israel on humanitarian grounds.

Citizenship: The 2011 amendment to the Nationality Law allows revocation of citizenship from a person on grounds of "breach of loyalty to the State of Israel." As of November 9, no one was stripped of his citizenship or permanent residence status. On May 29, Minister of the Interior Aryeh Deri filed a motion with the Haifa District Court to revoke the citizenship of Alaa Zayoud, whom the courts convicted of four counts of attempted murder in an October 2015 car-ramming attack. In addition, on June 26, Deri requested that the attorney general revoke the citizenship of Luqman Atun and the permanent residency of East Jerusalemite Khalil Adel Khalil, following their attempts to join Da'esh in Syria. All three motions were pending as of November 9.

On October 21, after the head of NGO B'Tselem called on the UN Security Council to take action to address the growth of Israeli settlements in the occupied territories, MK David Bitan, the chairman of the governing coalition, told media the remarks were an "explicit breach of trust by an Israeli citizen against the state, and as such he should find himself another citizenship." The government, however, did not take any steps to strip him of his citizenship.

Protection of Refugees

Access to Asylum: In 2008 authorities began giving the majority of asylum seekers a "conditional release visa" that requires renewal every one to four months. The government provided these individuals with a limited form of group protection with freedom of movement, protection against refoulement, and some informal access to the labor market. Access to health care, shelter, and education was available inconsistently. The protection environment, however, significantly deteriorated following the adoption in late 2011 of policies and legislation aimed at deterring future asylum seekers by making life difficult for those already in the country. These actions further curtailed the rights of the population and encouraged the departure of those already in the country.

The Refugee Status Determination (RSD) Unit of the Population Immigration and Border Authority handles asylum requests and publicizes information on how to apply in its offices and on its website. The RSD Unit set up a computer-based appointment system in Arabic and Tigrinya (Eritrean).

RSD recognition rates were extremely low. In the 2012-16 period, the government received 28,915 asylum applications, including 4,901 from Sudanese applicants, 7,848 from Eritreans, 7,130 from Ukrainians, and 4,221 from Georgians. Of those, according to the Ministry of Foreign Affairs, the government approved 27, denied 4,764, and closed 4,750 for other reasons such as departure from Israel or noncooperation. During the year the government approved only four asylum requests and denied 2,609. As of August, 326 requests submitted in 2009 were still pending, and as of the end of the year, 19,374 cases were pending, including 11,238 from Ukrainians and Georgians. While the government extended nonremoval and "conditional release visas" to a number of Sudanese from Darfur, it granted refugee status to a Sudanese applicant for the first time on June 21.

In addition to these low rates, according to international organizations, a lack of transparency in the documentation and deliberation phases of the government's processes further undermined confidence in the system, affecting views of the legitimacy of the government's regime for asylum seekers. HRM, the African Refugee Development Center, UNHCR, and the Tel Aviv University Refugee Rights Clinic expressed continuing concerns regarding the accessibility, efficiency, and impartiality of the RSD Unit.

Authorities originally granted this population protected status and barred them from applying for RSD, a policy later changed without notification to much of the population. Some of these individuals, however, applied through UNHCR upon arrival (and continued to have files with UNHCR that the government had not requested or accepted for transfer). Others were discouraged from applying by the government's policy summoning those who applied to detention in Holot and by the extremely low rate of acceptance of refugee claims.

In 2015 the government adopted a practice of requiring long-staying RSD applicants to provide an acceptable justification for not applying for RSD within their first year of residence in the country. The government then rejected the majority of justification applications from these individuals. In September an appeals tribunal ruled that asylum applications from Eritreans should not be rejected out of hand on the basis of fleeing military conscription. The Ministry of

Interior immediately appealed the ruling, and the case was pending as of the end of the year. In November another appeals tribunal overturned the government's blanket rejection of applications submitted more than one year after arrival. The government's response to the November ruling was pending as of November 10.

The government continued to give Eritreans and Sudanese outside of detention renewable "conditional release" documents, but recipients must renew these documents every one to four months. Only three Ministry of Interior offices in the country renew these visas. In 2015 authorities summoned 12,425 asylum seekers to Holot for a one-year detention period, although there were only 3,360 beds. NGOs reported that some asylum seekers failed to appear, while others reported to Holot after quitting their jobs and giving up their residence, only to learn that there was insufficient space at the facility. The Ministry of Foreign Affairs reported that authorities summoned 3,396 persons during the year.

In July the Be'er Sheva District Court ordered release of the asylum seeker held longest in prison, a man from Guinea detained in Saharonim Prison for 10 years. On August 23, authorities released him for one month on the condition that he depart the country. Data that HRM received under the Freedom of Information Law revealed that as of July 2015, there were 16 migrants detained for more than three years, 30 migrants detained between two to three years, and 31 migrants detained between one to two years.

Government officials and media outlets continued to refer to asylum seekers as "infiltrators" and characterized them as directly associated with increases in crime, disease, and vagrancy.

Refoulement: The government provided some protection against the expulsion or return of refugees to countries where their lives or freedom could be threatened and stated its commitment to the principle of nonrefoulement. During the year 465 irregular migrants and asylum seekers departed the country through a "voluntary return" program, compared with 3,381 in 2015 and 6,414 in 2014. The government provided most returnees with paid tickets to either Uganda or Rwanda, although those governments did not provide assurances of legal residency or the right to work, despite the Ministry of Foreign Affairs' claim that the receiving countries were obligated to allow the relocated individuals to stay and work. In 2015 a Be'er Sheva court upheld the legality of the secrecy of these agreements in response to a petition by NGOs. The government provided those departing a stipend paid in dollars of $3,400, and prior to departure, the Population and Immigration Authority and the Custody Review Tribunal reviewed mandatory recorded video interviews and written statements of those who opted to participate in the voluntary return program to verify they were departing voluntarily. The government claimed in September that there were no known cases of injury or harm to any of the relocated migrants after arrival in the receiving country and that they received all rights accorded in the agreements.

A coalition of NGO advocates for asylum seekers (including Amnesty International, HRM, and the African Refugee Development Center) questioned the government's policy of sending migrants to a foreign country. These groups were concerned that the destination countries were not prepared to care for the asylum seekers and considered that, in some cases, this transfer could amount to refoulement. Human Rights Watch (HRW) and other NGOs reported that the voluntary return policy led to many individuals returning to their country of origin via the foreign countries where they did not receive permission to stay upon arrival or where authorities did not meet their protection needs. In response to a petition by human rights groups, however, the government promised in November 2015 to expand monitoring of implementation of these agreements in the foreign countries, according to *Ha'aretz*. HRW and HRM documented the treatment of some returnees whom Sudanese and Eritrean authorities arrested upon their return to Sudan and Eritrea and whom those authorities reportedly surveilled, beat, threatened, and in some cases tortured. In November media reported that Sudan issued arrest warrants for 3,300 citizens who had returned from Israel. The Israeli government denied that anyone who left under one of these agreements had experienced refoulement, persecution, or harassment and affirmed that everyone had received the rights accorded to them under the terms of the agreements.

In March 2015 the government announced a new policy to deport migrants from Eritrea and Sudan by sending them to other countries in Africa. The government explained that this procedure would initially apply to those held in Holot (2,000 at the time) who either never applied for asylum or who had applied and been rejected. By November 2015 authorities had notified 43 persons that they must either depart from Israel to a country in Africa or go to prison indefinitely. NGOs filed a court case questioning the safety of this policy, and the Supreme Court decided that for the duration of the court case, those migrants affected could remain outside of jail. That month the Beer Sheva District Court ruled against the migrants and NGO petition, stating that the government may use its process for relocating migrants. The court recommended the government delay actual implementation until a process for monitoring those who travel is established. Following an appeal to the Supreme Court in March, the government submitted a confidential response regarding the agreements with African countries, which was partially revealed to the plaintiffs. The Tel Aviv University Refugee Rights Clinic stated that parts of the agreements are unwritten, the written portion does not include any supervision mechanism, the rights assured under the agreement include only the right to work and remain for an unspecified period of time, and there are no assurances of proper execution or sanctions for violation. As of the end of the year, no migrants were known to have been jailed under this policy.

The government stated it reached agreements with two foreign countries with regard to the relocation of migrants from Sudan and Eritrea, and the attorney general conditioned his approval of the relocation policy on the assurance of certain protections in those countries. According to UNHCR, if returned to their countries of origin, these individuals were likely to face major human rights abuses, including the risk of death, torture, and life imprisonment. According to the government, however, from 2010 to 2015, 12,300 migrants departed to safe foreign countries or to their country of origin voluntarily, with no cases of violations of the principle of nonrefoulement.

Freedom of Movement: UNHCR and NGOs expressed concern over the government's actions in providing protection and assistance to some refugees, asylum seekers, and other persons of concern, including victims of trafficking, but not to others. UNHCR and NGOs raised specific concerns over the government's use of so-called voluntary return of detained migrants, including those seeking asylum, as well as the government's failure to provide independent individual refugee status determinations for the vast majority of migrants of sub-Saharan African origin, including Eritreans and Sudanese. UNHCR and NGOs also raised objections and called for changes to the government's continued use of "anti-infiltrator" laws, which impose long-term detention on all individuals who enter the country irregularly. The amended Prevention of Infiltration Law gives authorities the discretion to detain these individuals for three months in prison followed by 20 months in an "open facility." In August 2015 the Supreme Court issued a provisional ruling on the Law to Prevent Infiltration that reduced the maximum time that the government may detain migrants in Holot from 20 to 12 months (see section 1.d.).

The government reported the arrival of 18 irregular migrants during the year, compared with 168 in 2015, and the departure of 3,088, including 792 under the "voluntary departure" program to a third country, as well as the departure of 325 asylum seekers, including 77 to a third country. The 18 irregular migrants who arrived in the year included 14 from Sudan, three from Turkey, and one from China.

The government reported the Holot facility was near capacity throughout the year, housing 2,892 asylum seekers as of September 21, in addition to 621 detainees in Saharonim and 99 in Givon. An amendment to the Prevention of Infiltration Law, passed in 2014, excluded from summoning to Holot all women and children, men who could prove that they have a wife or children in Israel for whom they provide, recognized trafficking victims, persons over age 60, and those whose health could be negatively affected by detention in Holot. According to UNHCR, as of April 2015, authorities can now send torture survivors to Holot; according to the Ministry of Foreign Affairs, the law exempts victims of human trafficking.

In 2015 the Ministry of Interior released four identified victims of torture from the Saharonim facility, three of whom had been in prison for four years, and granted 25 persons temporary stays of orders to the Holot facility in response to HRM petitions. The government asserted that it would not send men who have family living in the country to Holot. Regulatory procedures, however, forced many families to separate because male heads of household did not have proper legal documentation to prove their status as married with dependents and authorities; therefore, they were required to report to Holot. According to NGOs, these documentation problems often resulted when circumstances forced families to flee their countries of origin without important documentation, including marriage certificates. Some migrants and asylum seekers married locally but hesitated to register their relationship status due to fear of legal repercussions and due to authorities' not recognizing other marriages.

Employment: The few recognized refugees received renewable work visas. In 2015 many asylum seekers who once had B/1 work visas had this status downgraded, and most held a 2A5 visa, which explicitly reads, "This is not a work visa." The government allowed asylum seekers to work in the informal sector but not to open their own businesses or register to pay value-added tax, although the law does not prohibit these activities. In 2015 the Ministry of Interior conducted media campaigns to warn employers against hiring illegal foreign workers. Despite the lack of a legal right to employment, the government's published policy was not to indict asylum seekers or their employers for their employment.

Authorities prohibited asylum seekers released from the Holot facility from going to Eilat and Tel Aviv, in part to keep them from working there, and municipal officials in other areas stated they would oppose asylum seekers relocating to their communities. Nevertheless, media reported in 2015 that labor-recruitment companies sent representatives to Holot to interview those released for possible employment in hotels at the Dead Sea or elsewhere outside of Tel Aviv and Eilat.

The government reserves the right to demand unpaid value-added tax and levy substantial fines against business proprietors for operating businesses without a tax exemption. African asylum seekers in the Holot open facility may not work outside the facility, but some worked inside the facility for less than the minimum wage. Some of the facility's services depended on detainee labor. Some detainees erected stalls outside the facility to sell food or other goods, but authorities periodically demolished their kiosks based on sanitation concerns or the prohibition against employment.

The law bars migrants from sending money abroad, limits the amount they may take with them when they leave to the minimum wage for the number of months they resided in the country, and defines taking money out of the country as a money-laundering crime.

Access to Basic Services: Access to health care, shelter, and education was available on an inconsistent basis. Recognized refugees received social services, including access to the national health-care system, but the government did not provide asylum seekers with public social benefits such as health insurance. The government stated it provided infirmary services, including laboratory services, medical imaging, and general and mental hospitalization services in the Holot facility for individuals held there, including asylum seekers. UNHCR reported that when a detainee accessed health services, another detainee often provided translation, compromising confidentiality and potentially affecting the quality of treatment. The government sponsored a mobile clinic, and mother and infant health-care stations in south Tel Aviv, which were accessible to migrants and asylum seekers. The clinic provided health and dental services, sexually transmitted disease evaluation and treatment, and prenatal and infant medical care.

Two major providers of medical care for asylum seekers stopped providing nonurgent treatment in the summer. The Gesher clinic in Jaffa, which the Ministry of Health funded and was the only provider of mental health services to asylum seekers, announced in late July that it no longer would accept new patients. Ichilov Hospital in Tel Aviv, which had previously covered the cost of treatment of asylum seekers from its budget, ran out of funds in early August. The two remaining clinics in Tel Aviv, where most asylum seekers resided, offered only limited medical services.

<u>Temporary Protection</u>: The government provided temporary protection primarily to Eritrean and Sudanese asylum seekers. The Ministry of Interior continued to reject the applications of almost all Eritrean detainees, concluding that military desertion provided insufficient grounds for presenting a subjective fear of persecution and disregarding further evidence presented on conditions in Eritrea should individuals return. In September, however, an appeals tribunal ruled that applications from asylum seekers fleeing conscription in Eritrea cannot be rejected out of hand and must be adjudicated individually. The government immediately appealed the ruling, and the case was pending as of November 10.

Stateless Persons

Despite being eligible for Israeli citizenship since 1981, an estimated 20,000 Druze living in territory captured from Syria in 1967 largely refused to accept Israeli citizenship, and their status as Syrian citizens was unclear. They held Israeli identification cards, which listed their nationality as "undefined." Media reported that the number of Syrian Druze applying for Israeli citizenship had increased since 2011.

Section 3. Freedom to Participate in the Political Process

The law provides citizens the ability to choose their government in free and fair periodic elections held by secret ballot and based on universal and equal suffrage assuring the free expression of the will of the people.

Elections and Political Participation

<u>Recent Elections</u>: Observers considered parliamentary elections held in March 2015 free and fair. In 2014 a change in the law raised the electoral threshold from 2 percent of votes to 3.25 percent of votes, a move some civil society organizations criticized for its limitation on freedom of representation and its potential effect on parties representing the Arab minority. The four Arab-majority parties represented in the Knesset united into one faction, the Joint List, winning 13 seats and becoming the third-largest faction in the Knesset.

<u>Political Parties and Political Participation</u>: The Basic Laws prohibit the candidacy of any party or individual that denies the existence of the State of Israel as the state of the Jewish people or the democratic character of the state or that incites racism. Otherwise, political parties operated without restriction or interference. The Northern Islamic Movement, banned in November 2015, continued its practice of

prohibiting its members from running for local or national office and boycotting elections.

On July 19, the Knesset passed a law enabling dismissal of an MK for the remainder of the term if 90 of 120 MKs voted for expulsion, following a request of 70 MKs, including at least 10 from the opposition. The party of an expelled member could replace the MK with the next individual on its party list, and the expelled member could run in the next elections. The law was introduced in February after three Arab-Israeli MKs visited the parents of Palestinian terrorists and participated in a moment of silence to honor the slain terrorists. Opponents of the law in the Knesset and civil society claimed the government intended the law to target Arab legislators and that it harmed democratic principles such as electoral representation and freedom of expression.

On December 22, police arrested Joint List MK Basel Ghattas after he agreed to the removal of his parliamentary immunity to search and arrest. Authorities suspected him of smuggling cell phones and SIM cards to two Hamas-affiliated prisoners.

<u>Participation of Women and Minorities</u>: No laws limit the participation of women and members of minorities in the political process, and they participated in political life on the same legal basis as men or nonminority citizens. The law provides an additional 15 percent in campaign funding to municipal party lists composed of at least one-third women. Although senior political and social leaders often came from among veterans of the predominantly male officer corps, women participated widely in politics, including in leadership positions up to prime minister. Women faced significant cultural barriers in political parties representing conservative religious movements and the Arab minority, although the 2015 elections resulted in two female MKs from the Joint List winning seats. Following the 2015 elections, the 120-member Knesset had 29 female members and 15 Arab members. As of September the 21-member cabinet included four women, and one woman and one Druze were deputy ministers; there were no Arabs. For the first time, an Arab citizen of Israel, Aida Touma Suliman, chaired a permanent committee in the Knesset, the Committee on the Status of Women. Four members of the 15-member Supreme Court were women, and one was Arab.

In the lead-up to local council elections on November 29, the Be'er Sheva District Court in September overturned a decision by the Ministry of Interior to deny approximately 5,000 Bedouin residents in the al-Kasom Regional Council the right to vote because their identity cards showed their tribal affiliation instead of their place of residence.

In December, referencing Prime Minister Netanyahu's statement on election day in March 2015 that "Arab voters are going in droves to the polls," coalition whip MK David Bitan said, "I would prefer that the Arabs not go to the polls in droves and not go to the polls at all. It would be best if they did not vote."

Section 4. Corruption and Lack of Transparency in Government

The law provides criminal penalties for corruption by officials, and the government implemented these laws effectively. There were reports of government corruption, although impunity was not a problem.

Corruption: The government continued to investigate and prosecute top political figures. On September 18, police arrested more than 20 Balad party officials, including senior party members. The charges included concealment of millions of shekels in contributions from Israel and abroad. Balad MKs rejected the accusations as political persecution. The investigation continued as of November 1.

In September police arrested and placed under house arrest Netanya mayor Miriam Feirberg-Ikar on grounds of failing to disclose a financial interest relating to a luxury housing project. The investigation continued as of November 10.

The State Prosecutor's Office announced in September that it would summon former tourism minister Stas Misezhnikov for hearings before indicting him and 15 other members of the Yisrael Beitenu party on charges of corruption.

A police investigation into the National Transport Infrastructure Company, formerly known as the National Roads Authority, began in late 2015 and continued as of September. *Ha'aretz* reported that police recommended charging more than 40 suspects and 11 companies with corruption, including at least one former MK.

In April 2015 authorities convicted Rabbi Yeshayahu Pinto of bribing senior police officers in connection with an investigation of alleged fraud by a charitable organization he headed. As part of a plea bargain in which Pinto gave evidence against the head of the National Crime Unit, Police Commander Menashe Arbiv, he received a reduced sentence of one year in jail, which he began serving in

February, and a fine of one million shekels ($265,000). The investigation of Arbiv continued at year's end.

In May 2015 the government filed indictments against lawyer Ronel Fisher, retired police superintendent Eran Malka, former Tel Aviv district attorney Ruth Blum-David, and several business figures. Authorities variously charged the accused with taking and giving bribes, fraud and breach of trust, fraudulent receipt of assets in aggravated circumstances, money laundering, or obstruction of justice, each according to his or her role in the corruption affair. Authorities alleged retired police superintendent Eran Malka, a senior police officer in the Lahav 433 National Fraud Unit, was a key figure in the ring's obstruction of justice. In September 2015 authorities sentenced Malka to eight years in prison. The cases of Blum-David and Fisher continued as of November.

In December 2015 a Tel Aviv court indicted former Knesset member and minister for industry, trade, and labor, Benjamin Ben-Eliezer, on charges of bribery, fraud, breach of trust, money laundering, and tax evasion. Ben-Eliezer died on August 28, before the case concluded.

In May 2015 the Jerusalem District Court sentenced former prime minister Ehud Olmert to eight months in prison, following a conviction for fraud and breach of trust in the Talansky "cash envelopes" case. In December 2015 the Supreme Court ruled on Olmert's appeal of separate charges from 2014 in the "Holyland" affair, accepting his appeal of some charges but maintaining his sentence of 18 months in prison for bribery. Olmert began serving his sentence in February.

Financial Disclosure: Senior officials are subject to comprehensive financial disclosure laws, and the Civil Service Commission verifies their disclosures. Authorities do not make information in these disclosures public without the consent of the person who submitted the disclosure. There is no specific criminal sanction for noncompliance.

Public Access to Information: The law requires governmental agencies to make internal regulations, administrative procedures, and directives available to the public. Not all governmental agencies effectively implemented the law.

Section 5. Governmental Attitude Regarding International and Nongovernmental Investigation of Alleged Violations of Human Rights

Numerous domestic and international human rights groups operated without government restriction, investigating and publishing their findings on human rights cases. Government officials were generally cooperative and responsive to their views, and they routinely invited NGOs critical of the government to participate in Knesset hearings on proposed legislation. Human rights NGOs have standing to petition the Supreme Court directly regarding governmental policies and may appeal individual cases to the Supreme Court. A unit in the Foreign Ministry maintained relations with certain international and domestic NGOs.

Israeli and Palestinian NGOs, particularly those focused on human rights problems and critical of the government, asserted, however, that the government sought to intimidate and stigmatize them. On July 11, the Knesset passed a law requiring NGOs that received more than half their funding from foreign governments to state this fact in all their official publications, when they apply to attend a Knesset meeting, and in any communications with the public (on television, radio, billboards, or e-mails). The law was scheduled to take effect on January 1, 2017, with the first report due from NGOs to the Ministry of Justice in July 2018. The law fines NGOs that violate these rules 29,200 shekels ($7,700). The Ministry of Justice believed that 27 NGOs received more than half their funding from foreign governments; of these, 25 were human rights organizations. NGOs criticized the law as stigmatizing left-wing organizations, which more commonly received international funding from foreign governments, while rejecting similar requirements for those funded by private international donors, which was more common among right-wing organizations. The government claimed that the law facilitates transparency and the right of the public to know which governments actively funded NGOs and emphasized that the law does not place any limits on NGO funding, discriminate on the basis of political orientation, limit the activity of NGOs, restrict their freedom of association, or impose any additional financial obligations or sanctions.

Following an October speech by B'Tselem director Hagai El-Ad at the UN Security Council, calling for an end to the Israeli occupation of the West Bank, Justice Minister Ayelet Shaked accused him of "cooperating with our enemies in the political terror waged against us in the United Nations," and Tourism Minister Yariv Levin called for El-Ad to be imprisoned on the basis of "treason and providing aid to the enemy."

On October 27, the Knesset's Finance Committee approved renewal of Amnesty International Israel's tax reduction on donations for only one year, whereas most other NGOs were approved for three years. The Knesset press release stated that during the year, "the Tax Authority will reexamine the organization to determine whether it meets the legal criteria for receiving such a tax break and whether or not it operates in a manner that jeopardizes the country's security."

The Ministry of Interior continued to deny foreign nationals affiliated with certain pro-Palestinian NGOs and solidarity organizations entry into the country. Authorities required some foreign nationals to sign declarations stating their understanding that "all relevant legal actions" would be taken against them, "including deportation and denial of entry into Israel for a period of up to 10 years," if they traveled through the country to Palestinian Authority-controlled areas without appropriate authorization. The government stated it took this action on an individual basis, not according to the activities or platform of the NGOs with which these persons were affiliated.

The staff of NGOs, including B'Tselem, Israel Religious Action Center, and Breaking the Silence, received death threats, which spiked during periods government officials spoke out against their activities.

According to the Ministry of Defense, in 2015 the government increased enforcement of fines on Israeli arms exporters who broke the law, including a ban on exports to countries where genocide is occurring. Fines in 2015 totaled 2.8 million shekels (741,000), an increase of 40 percent from 2014.

The United Nations or Other International Bodies: The government generally cooperated with the United Nations and other international bodies. The government continued its participation in the UN Human Rights Council, including the Universal Periodic Review process, although it announced it intended to suspend all coordination with UNESCO in October following adoption of a resolution that omitted mention of the Jewish connection to the Temple Mount/Haram al-Sharif. Moreover, the government prevented the UN Human Rights Council's special rapporteur on the situation in the Palestinian territories occupied since 1967 from gaining access to the West Bank.

Government Human Rights Bodies: The state comptroller also served as ombudsman for human rights problems. The ombudsman investigated complaints against statutory bodies that are subject to audit by the state comptroller, including government ministries, local authorities, government enterprises and institutions, government corporations, and their employees. The ombudsman is entitled to use any relevant means of inquiry and has the authority to order any person or body to assist in the inquiry.

Section 6. Discrimination, Societal Abuses, and Trafficking in Persons

Women

<u>Rape and Domestic Violence</u>: Rape, including spousal rape, is a felony punishable by 16 years in prison, or up to 20 years' imprisonment for rape under aggravated circumstances or if the perpetrator rapes or commits a sexual offense against a relative. The government effectively enforced rape laws. On December 18, authorities granted former president Moshe Katsav parole after completing five years of a seven-year sentence for rape.

The government received 4,246 complaints of sex-related offenses and filed 760 indictments as of September 7, compared with 5,877 complaints and 1,133 indictments for all 2015.

As of December 15, husbands or partners killed nine women, and other family members killed seven women in what the government termed "murders due to family disputes" and women's rights groups termed "femicides." For example, Amna Yasin, who was in her ninth month of pregnancy, was stabbed to death on August 23. Authorities indicted her husband for murder. Arab and Jewish women's rights groups protested against what they perceived to be police inaction and societal indifference or support for such actions. The government stated that police had developed procedures and trained special investigators to deal with domestic violence, sex offenses, and the violation of protective orders in diverse communities, including the Arab community. NGOs, including Women Against Violence, Na'am, and The Abraham Fund Initiative, worked within Arab and mixed communities to counter femicide.

In February the IDF ordered all off-duty combat soldiers to carry their weapons, following a terrorist attack in the West Bank in which an unarmed soldier died. The Ministry of Public Security continued to allow armed security guards to take their weapons home at the end of their shifts, a practice reinstated in 2014 after the ministry prohibited it in 2013 when a coalition of NGOs raised concerns about the high rate of spousal killings by security guards using service weapons. The ministry announced strict regulations governing the storage of weapons at home and in public.

According to the Association of Rape Crisis Centers in Israel, the majority of rape victims did not report the crime to authorities due to social and cultural pressure.

Women from certain Orthodox Jewish, Muslim, Bedouin, and Druze communities faced significant social pressure not to report rape or domestic abuse. Experts in the field of social work and domestic violence prevention highlighted the reluctance of many Arab women to avail themselves of social services due to societal pressure and personal identification as Palestinians. In 2015 the government cooperated with The Abraham Fund Initiative on a pilot program to provide training for professionals in the field of domestic violence within the Arab community, bringing law enforcement officers, social workers, NGOs, and religious leaders together to coordinate services for survivors of domestic violence.

The Ministry of Social Affairs and Social Services operated 14 shelters for survivors of domestic abuse and a hotline for reporting abuse. In 2015 a total of 755 women used a shelter, an increase of 20 percent from 2014. Regulations allow women to stay in a shelter for up to a year. Two of these shelters were dedicated to the assistance of women from the Arab community, and authorities dedicated two others to caring for a mixed population of Arab and Jewish women. Approximately one-third of 103 centers for the prevention and treatment of domestic violence throughout the country operated in Arab communities or mixed Arab-Jewish cities. In 2015 the 103 centers fielded more than 14,000 cases of alleged abuse. The Ministry of Social Affairs and Social Services assisted women involved in prostitution, including emergency shelters, daytime centers, and therapeutic hostels.

Authorities established a special interministerial board headed by the deputy director general of the Ministry of Public Security to address the continuing problem of domestic violence. In 2014 the board presented interim findings and recommendations to the Committee for the Advancement of Women and Gender Equality in the Knesset.

<u>Other Harmful Traditional Practices</u>: According to a report by *Ha'aretz* in February, between 30 to 50 percent of Bedouin families in the Negev were polygamous. In August 2015 *Ha'aretz* reported that the justice minister and the attorney general announced, "Steps will be taken to enforce the law against polygamy," working collaboratively with social service providers. Some in the Arab community expressed concern these measures would negatively affect women and children financially, and they urged focusing the effort first on education and on the sharia courts that perform marriages. Others heralded the move.

Cases of domestic homicides of women continued to occur within the Arab community, contributing to a disproportionate number of killings of Arab women (see also Rape and Domestic Violence above).

Police conducted weekly assessments of threatened women to determine the level of threat and required protection and worked with government social welfare institutes and NGOs to safeguard threatened women.

<u>Sexual Harassment</u>: Sexual harassment is illegal but remained widespread. The law requires that authorities inform suspected victims of harassment of their right to assistance. Penalties for sexual harassment depend on the severity of the act and whether the harassment involved blackmail. Police notified all known victims of their right to receive assistance from the Association of Rape Crisis Centers in Israel. The law provides that victims may follow the progress on their cases through a computerized system and information call center. Authorities filed 223 indictments for sexual harassment in 2015 and 170 as of September 12. In 2015, however, the Central Bureau of Statistics conducted a poll for the Ministry of Public Security that indicated 98 percent of sexual harassment victims did not go to the police. In May a survey by Israel's Channel Two television station found that 28 of 32 female MKs had been sexually assaulted, including two after they had entered the Knesset.

Harassment based on gender segregation continued in some public places, including on public buses. A 2015 Beit Shemesh court ruled in favor of and awarded damages of 60,000 shekels ($16,000) to four local Orthodox women, who complained the municipality had not complied with a previous ruling to eliminate signs in public places requesting members of the public to dress modestly.

The Ministry of Transportation and Road Safety operated a 24-hour hotline to report complaints on public transportation, including segregation.

<u>Reproductive Rights</u>: Couples and individuals have the right to decide the number, spacing, and timing of having children; manage their reproductive health; and have access to the information and means to do so, free from discrimination, coercion, or violence. Traditional practices in Orthodox Jewish communities often led women to seek approval from a rabbi to use contraception.

Arab Israeli women, particularly from the Bedouin population, had limited access to health-care services and had poor indicators for illness, death, and life expectancy. In the unrecognized Arab Bedouin villages in the Negev, there were very few health-care facilities or medical services. According to PHR-I, there were only one-third of the doctors needed, a large lack of services, and need for proper infrastructure.

Discrimination: The law provides for the same legal status and rights for women as for men. In the criminal and civil courts, women and men enjoyed the same rights, but in some matters religious courts--responsible for adjudication of family law, including divorce--limited the rights of Jewish, Christian, Muslim, and Druze women. Women and men who do not belong to a recognized religious group faced additional discrimination. In August in response to a petition from women's rights organizations regarding the lack of female leadership in the religious establishment, the Supreme Court ordered the appointment of a female deputy director general of the Rabbinic Courts.

The law allows a Jewish woman to initiate divorce proceedings, but both the husband and wife must give consent to make the divorce final. Because some men refused to grant divorces, thousands of women could not remarry or give birth to legitimate children. In rare cases this rule happened in reverse, with women refusing to grant men divorces. Rabbinical tribunals sometimes sanctioned a husband who refused to give his wife a divorce, while also declining to grant the divorce without his consent.

A Muslim woman may petition for and receive a divorce through the sharia courts without her husband's consent under certain conditions, and a marriage contract may provide for other circumstances in which she may obtain a divorce without his consent. A Muslim man may divorce his wife without her consent and without petitioning the court. Through ecclesiastical courts, Christians may seek official separations or divorces, depending on their denomination. Druze divorces are performed by an oral declaration of the husband alone and then registered through the Druze religious courts, placing a disproportionate burden on the woman to leave the home with her children immediately. A civil family court or a religious court settles child custody, alimony, and property matters after the divorce, which gives preference to the father--unless it can be demonstrated that a child especially "needs" the mother.

Although the law prohibits discrimination based on gender in employment and wages and provides for class action antidiscrimination suits, a wage gap between men and women persisted. According to data published by the Central Bureau of Statistics in March 2015, a woman's median monthly income was 26.7 percent lower than a man's. The Knesset Research Center reported that in 2015, 32 percent of Arab women between the ages of 25 and 64 years old were employed, compared with 74 percent of Arab men and 80 percent of Jewish women. The government subsidizes daycare and afterschool programs to encourage labor participation by mothers and offers professional training to single parents.

The Authority for the Advancement of the Status of Women in the Prime Minister's Office works to mainstream women's participation in the government and private sector and to combat sexual harassment and domestic violence. The authority requires every city, local council, and government ministry to have an adviser working to advance women's issues. A government resolution requires ministers to appoint women to the directorates of government-owned companies until representation reaches 50 percent; according to a February report in *Calcalist*, six of 10 of the largest government-owned companies reached 50 percent. The law requires that at least one of two governmental representatives on the Committee for Appointment of Religious Judges be a woman; in July 2015 authorities appointed seven men and four women to the committee.

Discrimination in the form of gender segregation continued in some public places, including in public health clinics and at the Western Wall. The main plaza of the Western Wall has gender-segregated prayer areas where regulation prohibits women from leading prayers, singing aloud, or holding or reading from Torah scrolls. On January 31, following three years of negotiations, the cabinet passed an agreement to double the size of the non-Orthodox section immediately south of the main plaza, which was "administered with a pluralistic approach" and used by the Conservative Movement for prayer and ceremonies. The cabinet decision also called for creating a single entrance for all worshippers to replace the separate entrance used to access the non-Orthodox section. The government, however, delayed implementation of the agreement throughout the year, leading egalitarian-prayer NGOs such as the Women of the Wall to declare that the agreement had collapsed. On June 7, police briefly detained Lesley Sachs, the executive director of the Women of the Wall, for questioning on charges of breaching public order after she smuggled a private Torah scroll into the Western Wall plaza for use in an egalitarian prayer service. On November 2, in protest against government's failure to implement the January 31 agreement, leaders of the Conservative and Reform movements of Judaism joined the Women of the Wall in performing an act of civil disobedience by bringing 14 Torah scrolls to the women's section of the Western Wall.

According to media reports, in December 2015, at a conference in Bnei Brak, leading rabbis in the Ashkenazi ultra-Orthodox community issued an order to the principals of ultra-Orthodox institutions not to recognize the degrees of women who study in academic institutions. They also banned ultra-Orthodox women from attending colleges and universities, saying a woman's higher pay resulting from higher education was "a danger to the entire structure of the household."

In April the Reshet Bet radio station reported that hospitals in Tel Aviv and Jerusalem routinely segregated Jewish and Arab women in maternity wards, although not by official policy.

Children

Birth Registration: Children derive citizenship at birth within or outside of the country if at least one parent is a citizen. Births are supposed to be registered within 10 days of the delivery, and, according to the law, births are registered in the country only if the parents are citizens or permanent residents. Any child born in an Israeli hospital receives an official document from the hospital that affirms the birth, the mother's details, and the father's details as based on a joint declaration made by both the father and the mother. The country registers the births of Palestinians in Jerusalem, although Palestinian residents of Jerusalem reported delays in the process.

According to the National Council for the Child, 161,462 children in the country lacked Israeli citizenship and its corresponding rights; however, most of these children were not stateless because they were eligible for another citizenship or Palestinian passport. The council noted this number did not include the children of asylum seekers or irregular migrants. The figure included children of legal and illegal foreign workers and children of mixed marriages, especially those between Arab-Israelis and Palestinian residents of the occupied territories. The government stated that a child's status derives from a parent's status; if one of the parents is an Israeli citizen and the other is not, the child may be registered as Israeli as long as he or she lives with the parent who is an Israeli citizen or permanent resident.

According to UNHCR, the Ministry of Interior issues a Confirmation of Birth document, which is not a birth certificate, for children without legal residency status in the country, including children of asylum seekers, migrant workers, children of international students, and others who do not hold Israeli citizenship. At times the government refused to list the father's name or to give the child the father's last name on the Confirmation of Birth document. The Ministry of Interior requires parents without legal residency to sign a form declaring they are "present illegally" in the country before issuing this document. In response to a petition to require the government to issue an official birth document listing both parents' names, the Supreme Court ruled on June 1 that, until the government's transition to computerized hospital birth notices is complete, the Ministry of Interior should issue birth certificates showing all details listed in the Confirmation of Birth prepared by the hospital, including the father's name if declared at the time of the birth.

Education: Primary and secondary education is free and universal through age 17, and-compulsory through grade 12. The government implemented the Compulsory Education Law (integrating children ages three to five) in the 2015-16 school year.

The government did not enforce compulsory education in unrecognized Bedouin villages in the Negev, and Bedouin children, particularly girls, continued to have the highest illiteracy rate in the country. Preschool-age children in unrecognized Bedouin villages faced difficulty in transportation to the nearest preschool, which in some cases was more than six miles away. As a result more than 5,000 Bedouin preschool-age children did not attend a preschool, according to a March report from the Ministry of Education. The government does not grant construction permits in unrecognized villages, including for schools. On August 23, the Ministry of Education promised to phase in bussing for these preschoolers, as well as those in recognized towns, over the course of the 2016-17 school year with an additional allocation of 50 million shekels ($13 million).

The government operated separate public schools for Hebrew-speaking children and Arabic-speaking children. For Jewish children there were separate public schools available for religious and secular families. Individual families may choose a public school for their children to attend regardless of ethnicity. By law these two school systems receive government funding equivalent to public schools, although they do not consistently teach a basic curriculum, including math, sciences, humanities, and languages.

The government partially funded "recognized but not official schools," which are required to teach a corresponding percentage of the national curriculum and have greater administrative autonomy than public schools. In September 2015 schools in this category belonging to the Secretariat of Christian Schools went on strike to protest a cut in funding from the Ministry of Education, particularly as compared to the two politically affiliated ultra-Orthodox Jewish school systems. The government pledged to transfer an additional 50 million shekels ($13 million) by March 31, but as of December 9, the schools had received only one-quarter of that amount; negotiations continued. The government stated that it had dedicated additional resources to students living in the country's periphery and in disadvantaged communities that resulted in the addition of school hours, funding for formal and informal educational programs, and teacher enrichment in these communities.

The Tel Aviv municipality opened 46 new preschools and kindergartens and 10 first grade classes in September, primarily for the children of migrant workers and refugees, raising concerns of segregation, whether unintentional or deliberate. According to a July 28 report in *Ha'aretz,* the head of the city's education department claimed this pattern of assignments was primarily due to late registration by migrant families. Segregation by place of origin is illegal.

In recent years an influx of Arab residents to the primarily Jewish town of Nazareth Illit led to a significant population of Arab students with no option for education in Arabic; as a result most attended schools in Nazareth and nearby villages, despite paying municipal taxes in Nazareth Illit. In June ACRI submitted a petition demanding establishment of a school for Arabic-speaking students. The court instructed the Nazareth Illit municipality to reconsider the establishment of an Arabic school in the city and requested a response from the municipality by January 2017.

Medical Care: The government provides preventive health services to minors younger than age six without civil status. For noncitizens under age 18, it also provides services similar to those provided for citizens, regardless of their legal status in country, if their parents register them with the "Meuhedet" health-care fund. This arrangement does not include minors whose guardian is a resident of the Palestinian Authority, and it does not cover pre-existing conditions.

Child Abuse: The National Council of the Child received a number of complaints during the year of abuses related to health, availability of welfare services, education, physical and sexual abuse, child pornography, and poor educational environments.

The law requires mandatory reporting of any suspicion of child abuse. It also requires social service employees, medical and education professionals, and other officials to report indications that minors were victims of, engaged in, or coerced into prostitution, sexual offenses, abandonment, neglect, assault, abuse, or human trafficking. The government stated that police immediately attend to each case received from the National Council for the Child or any other source. Police maintained that they assigned officers with special training in dealing with child abuse without distinction to ethnic or racial background. NGOs, however, expressed concern regarding police negligence in child abuse and domestic violence cases reported in minority communities.

The government provided specialized training to psychologists, offered a free psychological treatment program to treat child victims of sexual offenses, and operated a 24-hour emergency hotline. The Ministry of Education operated a special unit for sexuality and for prevention of abuse of children and youth that assisted the education system in prevention and appropriate intervention in cases of suspected abuse of minors.

According to government data, minors were the victims in 47 percent of sex offenses in 2012-16. The most common offense against minors--77 percent of cases--was molestation. Approximately one-quarter of those complaints were for rape.

During March and April 2015, six children of migrants/asylum seekers died within five weeks. All six were in the supervision of workers in day-care centers that served the migrant/asylum seeker community and known to lack resources. Following the deaths the government announced it would allocate 56 million shekels ($14.8 million) to establish alternative day-care centers.

Early and Forced Marriage: The law sets the minimum age of marriage at 18 years old, with some exceptions for younger children due to pregnancy and for couples older than 16 years old if the court permitted it due to unique circumstances.

Sexual Exploitation of Children: The law prohibits sexual exploitation of a minor and sets a penalty of seven to 20 years in prison for violators, depending on the circumstances. In 2014 the Knesset amended the law to extend the prohibition on possession of child pornography (by downloading) to accessing such material (by streaming). The minimum age for consensual sex is 16 years old. Consensual sexual relations with a minor between the ages of 14 and 16 constitute statutory rape punishable by five years' imprisonment.

The government supported a number of programs to combat sexual exploitation of children, including an interministerial research team, preparing educational materials, and conducting numerous training sessions for government and police officials.

Until 2008 there was only one center for the protection of abused children in the country, located in Jerusalem, and its staff had no Arabic speakers. As a result of a petition brought by the National Council for the Child, in 2008 the Supreme Court ordered eight centers to open throughout the country within five years. As of 2015 the Ministry of Social Affairs and Social Services operated only six centers specializing in care of children and youths who experienced physical, sexual, or emotional abuse, or neglect by family members.

International Child Abductions: The country is a party to the 1980 Hague Convention on the Civil Aspects of International Child Abduction. See the Department of State's report *Annual Report on International Parental Child Abduction* at travel.state.gov/content/childabduction/en/legal/compliance.html.

Anti-Semitism

Jews constituted approximately 80 percent of the population. The government often defined crimes targeting Jews as nationalistic crimes relating to the overall Palestinian-Israeli conflict rather than anti-Semitism.

Trafficking in Persons

See the Department of State's *Trafficking in Persons Report* at www.state.gov/j/tip/rls/tiprpt/.

Persons with Disabilities

The Basic Laws provide a legal framework for prohibiting discrimination against persons with physical, sensory, intellectual, and mental disabilities in employment (including hiring, work environment, and evaluation), education, air travel and other transportation, access to health care, the judicial system, or the provision of other government services. The 1998 Equal Rights for Persons with Disabilities Law augments the Basic Laws and specifically prohibits discrimination against persons with disabilities, including with regard to public facilities and services. This legislation mandates access to buildings, information, communication, transportation, and physical accommodations and services in the workplace, as well as access to mental health services as part of government-subsidized health insurance.

In March the Knesset passed an amendment to the Legal Capacity and Guardianship Law. The reform moves toward greater legal empowerment of persons with disabilities, including recognition of supported decision making and enduring powers of attorney, reduction of cases in which guardians will be appointed as well as the scope of their powers, and definition of the rights of persons under guardianship.

In 2014 the Minister of Economy signed an order requiring that 3 percent of the workforce of employers with more than 100 employees be persons with disabilities. In August the Knesset passed a law requiring persons with disabilities hold at least 5 percent of jobs in government-funded bodies with 100 employees or more. According to NGOs, government progress in enforcing these laws was limited. Government agencies for persons with disabilities worked to encourage leadership from within the community of persons with disabilities and offered a subsidy for employers for the first three years of employment of a person with a disability.

Societal discrimination and lack of accessibility persisted in employment, housing, and education. According to the government's Commission for Equal Rights of Persons with Disabilities, the employment rate remained lower than that for persons without disabilities, and many persons with disabilities who were working had part-time, low-wage jobs. The government established a one-stop employment center for persons with disabilities during the year as a pilot project. The Ministry of Economy decreed that all sectors should increase their hiring so that persons with disabilities would constitute 3 percent of the workforce by the end of 2017, and the government continued to provide support and education for employers and workers with disabilities to close the gap. According to the commissioner for the rights of persons with disabilities, 100 percent of municipal buses and 60 percent of intercity buses were accessible, as of November 2015.

The disability rights NGO Bizchut reported that Arab citizens with disabilities were employed at approximately half the rate of Jews with disabilities. Shortages of funding for Arab municipalities, including for education, adversely affected Arabs with disabilities.

Access to community-based independent living facilities for persons with disabilities remained limited. According to Bizchut, more than 8,000 persons with intellectual disabilities lived in institutions and large hostels while only 1,500 lived in community-based settings. The Ministry of Social Affairs and Social Services moved 106 persons with intellectual disabilities from institutions into community-based housing facilities as part of a three-year pilot program that began in 2015.

The law prioritizes access by persons with disabilities to public services, such as eliminating waiting in line as well as providing adapted seating and accessible facilities in public places other than buildings, such as public beaches, municipal parks, swimming pools, and cemeteries. For hearing-impaired persons, the law provides for short-message public-announcement services.

The Commission for Equal Rights of Persons with Disabilities within the Ministry of Justice oversees the implementation of laws protecting the rights of persons with disabilities and worked with government ministries to enact regulations. The Unit for the Integration of Persons with Disabilities in the Labor Market, located within the Ministry of Economy, examined and promoted the employment of persons with disabilities. The unit had three support centers designed to assist employers who wish to hire persons with disabilities. The Ministry of Social Affairs and Social Services provides accommodation to persons with intellectual disabilities and/or autism who are either suspects or victims in criminal investigations.

Authorities hospitalized 24,000 persons in psychiatric hospitals each year, including 8,000 under involuntary hospitalization orders. According to a report published in March by Bizchut, psychiatric patients, including minors, faced excessive use of mechanical restraints of all four limbs. Patients were unable to move, even to scratch an itch or use the bathroom. Authorities restrained some patients for hours, others for days. The use of restraints was pervasive, with approximately 4,000 experiencing it at least once during their stay in 2014, often resulting in physical or psychological harm. The report found that the reason for restraint was often punishment or to control "nuisance" behaviors such as yelling or moving incessantly rather than any degree of danger. The Be'er Sheva Mental Health Center, which instituted an independent project to reduce the use of four-limb restraints, reduced the number of cases by 60 percent during the period 2014-15. During the year the Ministry of Health appointed a committee to investigate the use of restraints, which was scheduled to issue a report in January 2017.

National/Racial/Ethnic Minorities

The NGO Adalah maintained a database of more than 50 laws it claimed discriminated--either explicitly or in practice--against Arab citizens.

Arab citizens, many of whom self-identify as Palestinian, faced institutional and societal discrimination, particularly in the wake of a wave of terrorist attacks by individuals of Palestinian or Arab descent, which began in September 2015 and continued during the year. There were multiple instances of security services or other citizens racially profiling Arab citizens, as well as instances of revenge attacks directed towards or being carried out against Arabs.

In one case in October 2015, a 17-year-old Jewish Israeli stabbed four Arabs in the southern Israeli town of Dimona. When interrogated, he told police that his conviction that "all Arabs are terrorists" motivated him. Prime Minister Netanyahu condemned the attack. Authorities charged the attacker with four counts of attempted murder, and the case was pending as of the end of the year.

In January 2015 in Jerusalem, 10 Jewish assailants beat Tommy Hasson, a Druze veteran of the IDF, reportedly after they overheard him speaking Arabic. After police arrested several suspects, a judge found that assailants committed the attack with nationalistic motivations. The National Insurance Institute subsequently recognized Hasson as someone who survived "enemy hostilities." Nonetheless, in September police closed the investigation without charges due to "lack of evidence and the inability to fully identify the attackers."

There were no "price tag" attacks, which refers to violence by Jewish individuals and groups against non-Jewish individuals and property with the stated purpose of exacting a "price" for actions the government had taken against the group committing the violence. Attackers, however, invoked the term "price tag" in an incident that was a reaction to a terrorist attack by Palestinian individuals. In July the ISA arrested three minors on suspicion of burning cars and spray-painting in the village of Yafia one month earlier. According to police, two of the suspects admitted committing the vandalism as revenge for the June 8 terror attack at Sarona marketplace in Tel Aviv. Authorities indicted two of the minors for arson, malicious damage due to nationalistic motives, and obstruction of justice, and they indicted the third for failure to prevent a crime. The case continued as of year's end. The government classifies price tag attacks as terrorism. Since 2013 the Ministry of Defense--which has jurisdiction only over the West Bank and not inside the Green Line--has defined any association of persons that uses the term "price tag" as an illegal association. In prior years the most common offenses, according to police, were attacks on vehicles, defacement of real estate, harm to Muslim and Christian holy sites, assault, and damage to agricultural lands.

In June 2015 arsonists burned a large section of the Church of the Multiplication in Tabgha and scrawled on the building's stone walls sections of the Jewish prayer book that in this context denigrated Christians. In July 2015 the government announced five persons, including one minor, were responsible for the attack and filed indictments against two of them for aggravated arson, destruction of property due to hostility towards the public, conspiracy to commit a crime, and conspiracy for other acts, taking "administrative steps" against the other three. As of the end of the year, one of the suspects facing charges was under arrest and the other was under house arrest until the end of the court proceedings. The investigation also led to the sentencing of another suspect for two years' imprisonment on charges of sedition (possessing a publication that incites to violence or terror, according to the government). After initially declining to pay for repairs of the church, saying it did not fall under protections against acts of terror, the government agreed to pay 3.9 million shekels ($1 million) to restore the site. As of the end of the year, the government had transferred only 1.5 million shekels ($397,000), and negotiations continued for another 800,000 shekels ($212,000).

The law exempts Arab citizens, except for Druze men, from mandatory military service, but a small percentage served voluntarily. Those who performed military service received some societal and economic benefits; those who did not sometimes faced discrimination in hiring. Citizens generally are ineligible to work in companies with defense contracts or in security-related fields if they have not served in the military. Some Druze and a small number of Jewish conscientious objectors opposed inclusion in mandatory military service, and authorities sometimes jailed them for refusing to serve.

The government managed a National Civil Service program for citizens not drafted for military service, giving Arabs, some ultra-Orthodox Jews, Orthodox Jewish women, and others the opportunity to provide public service and thus be eligible for the same financial benefits accorded military veterans. Many in the Arab community opposed the National Civil Service program because it operated under the auspices of government ministries associated with security. There were also multiple instances of ultra-Orthodox communities ostracizing ultra-Orthodox soldiers for serving in the military. In November 2015 the Knesset voted to extend deadlines for mandatory conscription of men in the ultra-Orthodox community until 2020.

In December 2015, following negotiations with the Arab community, the cabinet approved a five-year plan for development of the Arab sector in the fields of education, transportation, commerce and trade, employment, and policing. The resolution pledges as much as 15 billion shekels ($3.9 billion), including mandated percentages from each ministry's budget, to increase economic integration and reduce societal gaps among Arab citizens over five years. It excluded mixed Jewish-Arab cities, such as Lod and Ramle, and unrecognized Bedouin villages. The plan is under the supervision of the Authority for Economic Development of the Arab Population in the Ministry of Social Equality. The Arab community welcomed the plan's adoption, albeit with skepticism that the authorities would fully implement it. On August 25, the Ministry of Construction and Housing announced agreements with 15 Arab localities for planning "hundreds of housing units and commercial zones" in the first implementation of the plan. The government earmarked more than 2.1 billion shekels ($550 million) to be used during the year, and most of these allocations were distributed to the relevant government authorities. These included 424 million shekels ($112 million) for transportation and infrastructure improvements, 91 million shekels ($24 million) to expand higher education opportunities, and 215 million shekels ($57 million) for the development of industrial areas and support of small- and medium-sized businesses. The Ministry of Foreign Affairs stated that the minister for social equality instructed the Economic Development Authority to monitor the activities of each office allocated money under this plan and provide for efficient implementation.

During the year authorities continued implementing earlier allocations including: a resolution from 2014, which budgeted 664 million shekels ($175 million) for improving infrastructure in Arab localities, including transportation, water and sewage, tourism, industrial areas, vocational training, sports halls, and personal security; and a resolution from 2013, which allocated 54 million shekels ($14 million) for improving education, employment, health services, and infrastructure in Druze localities in the Golan Heights.

In a 2014 study, the NGO Sikkuy found that the main cause of unequal resources for many Arab local authorities, including high schools, was their low tax base, requiring central government investment in economic and social development. The government initiated and continued several programs to support disadvantaged populations and periphery communities in general and the Arab community in particular.

The government employed affirmative action policies for persons of Arab descent, including members of Druze communities, and for non-Arab, Muslim Circassian communities, in the civil service. According to the Ministry of Foreign Affairs, as of the end of the year, there were 4,000 non-Jewish employees in the civil service. The Education Ministry continued implementing a plan to place 500 Arab teachers in positions in predominantly Jewish schools by 2020. The plan offered partial solutions for many Arabs with teaching credentials who could not find work as teachers and for Hebrew-language schools that experienced a shortage of teachers in key subject areas including math, English, and science. As of August there were

588 Arab educators teaching in Jewish schools, according to the news outlet Israel Hayom. Out of 24,000 participants at employment centers designed for unemployed Arab, Druze, and Circassian men and women, 13,600 became employed from 2012 to 2015.

Separate school systems within the public and semipublic domains produced a large variance in education quality, with Arab, Druze, and ultra-Orthodox students passing the matriculation exam at lower rates than those of their non-ultra-Orthodox Jewish counterparts. The government noted that the Ministry of Science and Technology and the Ministry of Education operated programs to provide free matriculation-exam coaching to Arab students. According to the Central Bureau of Statistics, the percentage of students in Israel in 2015-16 who were Arab was 14.3 percent in undergraduate programs, 11.7 percent in master's programs, and 6 percent in PhD programs. While these percentages were lower than the Arab percentage of the country's total population, they were higher than the percentages in 1999-2000 (9.8 percent, 3.6 percent, and 2.8 percent, respectively). The government operated several scholarship programs specifically targeting the Arab population, including 650 scholarships valued at 10,000 shekels ($2,600) per year each for Arab students enrolled in a first-degree program. Statistics researched by *Ha'aretz--TheMarker* and the Knesset research center found that Arab students received slightly higher per-capita government support than their non-ultra-Orthodox Jewish peers. Two ultra-Orthodox school systems continued to benefit from higher funding percentages than all other school systems. Mossawa claimed that Arab schools faced a shortage of up to 3,000 classrooms as of August. According to the Ministry of Foreign Affairs, in December 2015 the Council for Higher Education invited proposals for the establishment and operation of a state-funded college in an Arab locality in northern Israel.

Representation of Arabs and the Arabic language in Israeli media was far less than their proportion in the population. Mossawa reported that two Israeli television stations, Channels Two and 10, used less than 0.5 percent of their annual budget for Arab programming, and only 2 to 3 percent of experts interviewed in Israeli media were Arabs. There was only one licensed Arabic radio station, based in Nazareth, but 16 Arabic stations broadcast without licenses. On May 8, the government passed a resolution instructing government offices to increase the diversity of the individuals shown in their advertisements and other publications.

In November the Ministry of Transportation removed automated audio announcements in Arabic from urban busses in Be'er Sheva after receiving complaints from the mayor and residents shortly after the announcements began. Busses continued to display electronic announcements in Arabic and Hebrew.

Approximately 93 percent of land is in the public domain, including approximately 12.5 percent owned by the NGO Jewish National Fund (JNF), whose statutes prohibit sale or lease of land to non-Jews. Following a 2004 lawsuit filed by human rights organizations, the attorney general ruled in 2005 that the government may not discriminate against Arab citizens in marketing and allocating lands it manages, including those of the JNF. The human rights organizations withdrew their petition on January 27 after the Israel Lands Administration (ILA) and JNF made a new arrangement in which Arab citizens will be allowed to participate in all bids for JNF land, but the ILA will grant the JNF another parcel of land whenever an Arab citizen of Israel wins a bid. The NGO Adalah, one of the petitioners in the case, noted that this arrangement solves the specific problem of discrimination in JNF bids but not the underlying ethnonational bias behind the policy.

New construction was illegal in towns that did not have an authorized outline plan for development, which is the legal responsibility of local authorities. Arab communities that still lacked fully approved planning schemes could turn to their municipal authorities to develop them, according to the government. The government stated that as of August 2015, 131 of 133 Arab localities had approved outline plans for development, 84 of which the National Planning Administration furthered. It stated that outline plans advanced by the Ministry of Interior added an average of 70 percent to existing localities' lands and noted that delays in the approval of plans often related to the lack of vital infrastructure such as sewage systems. The government noted that a government decision in July 2015 includes multiple provisions on the subject of housing problems in Arab localities. On August 25, the Ministry of Construction and Housing announced agreements with 15 Arab localities for planning "hundreds of housing units and commercial zones."

NGOs serving the Arab population, however, alleged discrimination in planning and zoning rights, noting regional planning and zoning approval committees did not have Arab representation, and planning for their areas was much slower than that for Jewish municipalities, leading frustrated citizens to build or expand their homes without legal authorization and risk a government-issued demolition order. A "Target Price" housing program of the ILA, designed to reduce the cost of housing by as much as one-fifth of the national average price, did not include Arab municipalities. Additionally, some communities discriminated against Arabs. Adalah alleged in 2015 that an association that won a tender to market new